KU-206-997

Floating Collections

Floating Collections

A Collection Development Model for Long-Term Success

Wendy K. Bartlett

 LIBRARIES UNLIMITED

AN IMPRINT OF ABC-CLIO, LLC
Santa Barbara, California • Denver, Colorado • Oxford, England

Copyright 2014 by Wendy K. Bartlett

All rights reserved. No part of this publication may be reproduced, stored in a retrieval system, or transmitted, in any form or by any means, electronic, mechanical, photocopying, recording, or otherwise, except for the inclusion of brief quotations in a review, without prior permission in writing from the publisher.

Library of Congress Cataloging-in-Publication Data

Bartlett, Wendy K.
  Floating collections : a collection development model for long-term success / Wendy K. Bartlett.
    pages cm
  Includes bibliographical references and index.
  ISBN 978–1–59884–743–7 (pbk. : acid-free paper) — ISBN 978–1–59884–744–4 (ebook)
1. Cooperative collection development (Libraries)—United States. 2. Public libraries—Collection development—United States. I. Title.
Z687.15.B37 2014
025.2′1—dc23   2013033820

ISBN: 978–1–59884–743–7
EISBN: 978–1–59884–744–4

18 17 16 15 14   1 2 3 4 5

This book is also available on the World Wide Web as an eBook.
Visit www.abc-clio.com for details.

Libraries Unlimited
An Imprint of ABC-CLIO, LLC

ABC-CLIO, LLC
130 Cremona Drive, P.O. Box 1911
Santa Barbara, California 93116-1911

This book is printed on acid-free paper ∞

Manufactured in the United States of America

For Dad and Mum, and of course, Evan

Contents

Acknowledgments

I would like to acknowledge the many librarians, directors, shelvers, and circulation clerks to whom I spoke in the course of researching this book, named and unnamed within these pages, who took the time to speak with me or answer emails, all in the name of making it easier for the next library.

A huge thanks to the following libraries for their unwitting hospitality during the writing of this book on my off days, vacations, and evenings: the Medina County District Library's Medina branch, the Orrville Public Library, and the Rocky River Public Library. You made me feel very much at home and then left me alone to write. Bless you and your warm and welcoming libraries!

A special thanks to my colleague and friend Melissa Barr, for her copy-editing, research, and encouragement; to Cindy Orr for her friendship, tutoring, and generosity, both in sharing her original list of floating library systems and for pointing me in the right direction; to Sari Feldman, for making innovation the expectation every day at Cuyahoga County Public Library; and to Tracy Strobel for convincing me this was a book, not just an article. And finally, a huge thanks to my editor, Barbara Ittner, for her excellent suggestions, editing, and patience. Thanks, all!

Introduction to Floating Collections

In 1930, a Carnegie library system was created in the Canadian Northwest, and the Fraser Valley Regional Library system was born. The first regional library in North America, Fraser Valley is situated in a ruggedly beautiful area of British Columbia a few hours east of Vancouver. Because the Great Depression was in full swing as the new library system opened its doors, cost-saving measures were the watchword in Fraser Valley from the very beginning. If a patron braved the elements and returned a book to a branch other than the one from which he or she had borrowed the book, there was no question about spending valuable resources to return it to the "owning" branch, which might be miles away across challenging terrain. Housing the collection took a back seat to the practical matters of maintaining a functioning library system with nearly nonexistent funding. And the library system in Fraser Valley sprawled over a large geographic area during an era that predated a modern highway system by a couple of decades.

And so, more than 80 years ago, the first floating library collection was born. Sharing the collection and letting it live wherever it landed was just good, solid, Canadian common sense. For many of the Canadian regional systems, floating originated not as an innovative approach to housing their collections but as an organic outcome of serving patrons in geographically challenging areas on limited budgets. From the beginning, floating collections saved money and time.

Today, floating is a popular organizational model for public libraries. Simply defined, a floating collection is a system-wide collection wherein there is no owning branch designation. An item checked out from one branch and returned to a different branch stays at the branch to which the item was returned. Items are not rerouted back to an owning or originating collection as they would be in a traditionally housed collection. Instead, items "stay where they land" and are shelved as part of that return branch's collection. "Floating" has become the standard word for this type of collection (although early innovators also referred to this system as "decentralized" or "shared"). Materials are purchased (and weeded) with an eye toward how they will perform in the entire system, not at particular branches. Floating collections are rapidly becoming a standard best practice in public library systems large and small across North America. The Public Library Association's (PLA) conference in 2010 featured both a preconference session and a panel discussion focused on the implementation of floating collections as floating established itself firmly in the mainstream.

WHY FLOATING WORKS FOR TODAY'S LIBRARIES

Floating has emerged as an attractive option for contemporary libraries for one very simple reason: it saves money. For many years floating was regarded as just an intriguing alternative model. In recent years, severely reduced budgets have motivated library administrators to implement floating as a cost-cutting measure, helping them to realize savings in delivery costs, labor, and collection budgets. Materials are handled less, meaning fewer trips back to owning locations and fewer loads for drivers and trucks. Reduced handling saves wear and tear on hundreds of thousands of items. Clerks at circulation desks eliminate several steps as the need for routing books back to the owning location becomes unnecessary, saving precious labor hours. And collection budgets can benefit, because not every branch must have a copy of every potentially in-demand item. Items can go where they are needed and wanted, creating an efficiency over the "just-in-case" model of a traditional collection, wherein items are purchased for every branch, large or small, on the chance a patron might want them.

A WORD ABOUT EBOOKS

The introduction of eBooks to libraries has had long-reaching effects. How does the rise of eBooks bear on floating collections? First and foremost, as many eBook-reading patrons prefer bestsellers, eBooks do help to cut down on the number of multiple copies of hardback bestsellers that must be repurposed. But unless collection development budgets allow for large numbers of eBook copies to be purchased, this effect is minimal. However, one very big gain for eBooks is that with money saved by floating, collection development dollars could potentially be invested to grow that particular collection. Otherwise, eBooks live a separate life from the collections that floating will affect.

IT IS NOT ALL ABOUT THE MONEY

A surprising secondary effect of floating occurred for most floating systems. Because hot items did not spend hours on delivery trucks, and because collections were refreshed daily as a result of patron activity, circulation went up. Patrons play a role in what items land where, fine-tuning the collection to meet the needs of the community in ways collection development librarians can only dream of. And hot items get back in patrons' hands faster, resulting overall in happier patrons and higher circulation.

WHY A BOOK ON FLOATING COLLECTIONS?

This book came into being for two reasons. Many library systems are considering floating or have decided to float but do not really know how to get started. Given the groundswell of popularity floating has enjoyed in recent years, a review of the literature reveals surprisingly little published on the topic. Most libraries learn to float from other libraries that have done it, passing information about the experience from one system to another. This book attempts to pull together existing information about floating, documents some of the best practices emerging from library systems with floating collections, and discusses the common hard-to-solve issues that floating engenders.

This book is also for those librarians involved with collection development and maintenance who already live with a floating collection and the collection management challenges it can present. Unless the stars are aligned perfectly most floating library systems will have a small percentage of branches that are "heavily hit" branches overloaded by patron returns. A smaller percentage of branches will be "have-nots": those branches where patrons shop heavily but return items elsewhere, stripping the shelves of desirable materials. The longest-lasting unpleasant reality for a small number of branches in floating library systems is unquestionably the rebalancing problem. This book will look at what some libraries have done to address this problem and explore why there is no one right answer to this very real daily hassle for floating library systems.

Likewise, this book will look at other challenges that arise when floating is implemented. How do collection development librarians purchase differently? Weed differently? Budget differently? How about maintaining a core collection in this brave new world that changes every hour of every day? And what to do about multiple copies that just will not go away? This book examines how libraries across the United States and Canada have responded to these challenges.

This book will explore

- what a floating collection is and all the various forms floating can take;
- how floating works and how to get it started;
- what librarians need to consider before, during, and after a floating collection is launched;
- what sound collection management practices can do to maximize the advantages of floating and minimize the disadvantages; and

- how to understand what patrons are telling us about what they want through observing and analyzing patron activity in a floating collection.

Librarians in systems who have already floated agree that there is precious little guidance out there on how to float, still less on what happens to the collection once floating begins. Those librarians are accustomed to a steady stream of phone calls and emails asking for guidance, coming from decision makers at library systems poised on the brink of floating. Most fledgling floaters rely on the kindness of the library community and their colleagues who have "been there, done that" to guide them. But what works for the library across the state (or indeed, across the country) may not work for every library.

This book will define floating collections, address the advantages and drawbacks, outline a how-to process to prepare a collection (and a staff!) for floating, and give guidance on how to cope with issues that arise once a collection is up and floating. This book is intended for anyone involved in the decision making process before, during, and after launching a floating collection. Administrators and board members will benefit from the overview and pros and cons. Managers in branches, technical and information services, and circulation departments will find material relevant to their areas of responsibility in terms of preparing and launching a floating collection. And librarians working with selection, weeding, or any aspect of collection development or management will find it most helpful both in planning for floating a collection and for coping with a floating collection after the fact.

In preparing this book, a comprehensive view of the literature was conducted; relevant articles and other sources are included in the bibliography. Surveys as well as phone and email interviews were conducted with librarians across the United States and Canada, and their answers were synthesized with published works in an attempt to put the collective wisdom on floating collections at the reader's fingertips.

ORGANIZATION

This book does not have to be read from beginning to end. It is arranged so that the reader can make the most effective use of the material. Readers trying to understand what a floating collection is and whether it is right for their system will want to start at the beginning. Librarians who have decided to move forward with floating but would like a "how-to" can skip to the relevant sections. Librarians who are already working with a floating collection and may be experiencing problems with selection, core collections, or weeding can turn to those chapters. Different sections will be relevant at different times during the process.

METHODOLOGY

This book blends approaches of many libraries and identifies best practices of many systems. Some of the librarians interviewed have worked with floating collections for over 20 years. Some are initiating floating as we speak, and the rest are somewhere in between those two extremes. Questions posed to these individuals were: What would they have done differently? What changes has floating wrought to the collection a decade later? And most importantly, what best practices have been developed?

The results of those conversations will help to fill the information gap on floating in several ways. This book will

- examine floating in such a way as to help nonfloating systems decide whether or not floating is right for them;
- discuss common roadblocks to successful floating and how to best overcome them based on the collective experience of library systems that have gone before;
- demonstrate simple methods with which systems can predict how the float will impact their particular situation, branches, staff, and collections;
- outline a step-by-step method for floating a collection with optimum results;
- discuss long-term advantages and challenges to collection development work once a collection has floated.

This book will cover issues of interest to everyone from library directors to trustees to staff members, at all levels and in every department, as floating affects literally every part of a system's operation. Collection development, branch and technical services, circulation staff, shelvers, and delivery staff members are all affected by floating in different ways, and each can draw on different sections of this book to help them when the time comes to make decisions about floating. Librarians in systems that are gearing up to float will find this book most helpful in planning for their transition, predicting its impact on their collection and branches, and putting solutions in place before issues arise, in order to better cope with the imbalances and other issues floating brings. In systems that are currently floating, librarians who are still trying to cope with collection imbalances, staff resistance, or other artifacts of floating will find this book helpful as they can learn of solutions arrived at by other systems.

COMMON CONCERNS THAT ARE ADDRESSED

Is it possible to float only parts of the collection, rather than the whole thing? (Chapter Two)

What happens if too many items end up at one branch? What happens if the main library is drained and loses inventory? (Chapter Six)

How should communication with staff and staff concerns be handled? (Chapter Four)

What is the best way to select for a floating collection? (Chapter Seven)

Will our collections lose their unique identity? (Chapter Seven)

What will our patrons think? (Chapter Seven)

What will happen to our smallest branch? (Chapter Three)

What steps are needed to float a collection? (Chapter Five)

Chapter One looks at the history of floating. (It has been around since the Great Depression!) The chapter also examines what kinds of libraries float and what kinds do not, also exploring under what circumstances, if any, libraries have stopped floating and returned to a traditionally housed collection.

Chapter Two examines the questions that decision makers must ask themselves when deciding whether or not to float their collection. And once the decision to float has been made, what parts of the collection should float? What other technical and philosophical decisions need to be made before beginning?

Chapter Three is all about prediction. Readers will learn how to predict what will happen with floating, using very basic and easily obtainable metrics. Floating will create a collection imbalance; readers will learn how to predict where and to what degree this will occur.

Chapter Four is devoted to communication with staff members: who needs to know what, and when. A suggested timeline for prefloat and postfloat communication is included.

Chapter Five offers valuable practical advice on preparing the collection for floating, from cleaning up the shelving workflow to weeding.

Chapter Six walks the reader through the process of dealing with problems once floating begins. How do "heavily hit" branches cope with the influx? How do the "have-nots" regain inventory? Do vendors have a practical solution for rebalancing and managing floating collections?

Chapter Seven is intended for those librarians tasked with solving long-term collection development and management issues, such as weeding, selection, budgeting, maintaining a core collection, and long-term communication and feedback with branch staff members.

Floating a collection is a major decision; even more, it is a major operational undertaking—yet there are great advantages to a floating collection that merit serious consideration. No library system that has seriously undertaken floating has yet to return to a traditionally housed collection. Many of the collection development librarians and administrators of those floating systems have contributed their suggestions and cautions to this book, in order that those who follow can be spared "learning the hard way" about the nuances and ramifications of floating. Still worried? Read on!

CHAPTER ONE

The History of Floating Collections

In the nascent years of floating, the main reason for a library to go to a floating collection was often the geographical size of the library system, which is why so many pioneers of floating are to be found in Canada and the Western United States. Floating collections were a way to work around adverse weather conditions and mitigate miles of delivery routes that, in many cases, became impassable in winter. But floating brought other positive side effects. First, it saved library systems a considerable amount of money, both operationally (reduced handling and delivery) as well as in collection development budgets. Soon floating began to creep eastward from the Rocky Mountains and westward toward California. But for several decades, floating collections were a well-kept Rocky Mountain secret.

Then in October of 2004, Ann Cress, then of Jefferson County Public Library in Jefferson County, Colorado, penned a landmark article for *Library Journal*, titled "The Latest Wave," that brought floating to the attention of the larger library world. In that article, Cress credits both Pikes Peak Library District in Colorado and Fraser Valley Regional Library in British Columbia for originating floating. Both Pikes Peak and Fraser Valley had been floating for many years at the time of Cress's article. Sally Houghton, the collection development manager for Pikes Peak Library District, confirms that their library collection has been floating for over 20 years (Houghton, interview).

Then how is it that floating stayed out of the mainstream for so long? For one thing, for many libraries money was relatively plentiful in the 1990s.

Because floating saves money, it is not surprising that it comes to the fore more often during economic hard times than prosperous ones. Secondly, soon after the quiet inception of floating by these two library systems, another major change swept the library world: namely, the advent of the integrated library system (ILS). As computerizing catalogs and technical services functions became not a trend but a necessity, librarians' attention focused for years on vendors, training, and implementation above all else. The library world was fixated for a decade or more on achieving the smoothest transition possible to the integrated library system that best served them and their patrons. Therefore collection management innovations like floating had to meet one important criterion: they had to function along with the integrated library systems.

In the mid-1990s, decades after Pikes Peak and Fraser Valley had implemented floating collections, other libraries became interested but faced one major hurdle: the integrated library systems did not offer a floating option. Once Innovative Interfaces, Inc., (also known as Triple I) and other major vendors were convinced that a floating option was a good investment, changing a traditionally housed collection to a floating one could happen with a flip of a switch. Once the major vendors of integrated library systems were able to accommodate floating, the rest was history. Without floating becoming viable within an ILS framework, it would have remained a curiosity, not the emerging best practice it has become today.

FLOATING COLLECTIONS

Essentially, a floating collection is a system-wide collection wherein there is no "owning" branch designation. "Floating" has become the standard word for this type of collection, although early innovators also referred to this system as "decentralized" or "shared." When items in a floating collection circulate, they are shelved wherever they are returned by the patron instead of being routed back to an owning location. If a patron takes an item from Branch A and returns it to Branch B, it stays at Branch B as part of that branch's collection until such time as it is moved (floated) to the next location by a patron's action (such as a hold or return). If a patron requests a book from the main library be sent to her neighborhood branch, then returns that book to that same neighborhood branch, it is not sent back to the main library but stays where it was returned. Similarly, if a patron requests an item to be sent to his neighborhood branch but fails to pick it up, that item is not taken from the hold shelf and rerouted back to the owning branch. It is taken from the hold shelf and simply shelved as part of that branch's collection.

This change in location is reflected in the library's catalog. When the item is checked in upon return, the floating module in the ILS changes that item's location to match the location where it is being checked in. This is the first paradigm shift for library staff members. In a traditionally housed collection, staff members often come to think of the items housed at their branch as "their" books. The idea that "their" books will float away is a very disconcerting notion. Fortunately this particular staff concern is one that dissipates quickly once floating begins. For one thing (and this will be stressed repeatedly throughout this book), the greater the circulation of a format or section of the collection (such as DVDs, popular new books) the higher the rate at which that format or type floats. Entire branch holdings do not float away overnight. Staff members will see their copies of popular films or books float away in the first few days of floating, yes. However, they will also see other copies of the same types of materials float right in. After a few weeks, staff members begin to trust that the float will bring them what they need.

It is not complicated. One library board member referred to it as the "stuff-stays-where-it-lands" system, and that pretty much says it all. Floating *is* simple, elegantly so, in principle. But in reality, floating brings tremendous challenges (as well as benefits!) to libraries and library collections. Some of those challenges are extreme but short term, and if planned for and dealt with quickly, the transition to floating can be a smooth one. For those staff members working with specialized collections, or those who have spent their careers tending a main library's carefully curated collection, floating can be traumatic.

There are two solutions for these staffers. First, not all libraries float the entire collection. A specialized collection can be identified as such and the codes for that collection can be left in "nonfloat" mode in the ILS. Secondly, a possible solution is to not float all or part of the main library's collection. However, fewer materials floated means less money saved. In most cases, librarians become accustomed to the idea that it is their specialized knowledge that serves the library, even though the specialized collection now lives throughout the system rather than under one roof.

There are two very immediate consequences from floating. Circulation staff and delivery drivers escape the repetitive jobs of rerouting hundreds of items a day and delivering them to their owning locations. Because of this, popular items do not spend time riding around in trucks but are immediately available to be checked out by the next customer. This increased availability of inventory gives an immediate boost to circulation and engenders positive comments from patrons. For the same reason—less time spent on delivery trucks—there is less need to buy as many multiple copies of bestsellers as are needed in a traditionally housed collection. The copies a library has are available at all times except when a customer has actually checked the copy out or has it on hold. This immediacy and increased availability helps to save money for collection budgets.

HOW THE FLOAT BEHAVES—AND MISBEHAVES

There is no question that floating affects collection development beyond the initial implementation stage. The good news is that there is almost immediately more money for the library's collection development staff to spend, as floating collections can make fewer copies go farther. Most systems wholeheartedly agree that in the long run they save on collection budgets when they float. But without a stable collection that staffs tend daily, the challenge of maintaining a solid core collection can be a daunting one. Floating forces collection development staff to really think about what kind of collection is right for their entire library system, as floating mercilessly reveals the poorly weeded (or poorly selected) collection in a hurry. Despite all the challenges, decision makers continue to make the changeover to floating collections, unable to resist the compelling budget savings.

For the majority of branches, floating becomes a nonevent a week or two after floating begins. Materials leave, materials float in. The collection looks refreshed and attractive. With reasonably diligent weeding and shelving practices, there is plenty of shelf space consistently opening up to provide a home for materials floating in. Those happy branches tend to be in the middle of the bell curve: medium-sized, with a medium level of circulation, and in a moderately busy area—not on a major commuter route or hidden away in a quiet bedroom community.

It is very important when considering a move to a floating collection to remember that the majority of branches do just fine. Rebalancing issues with those branches at the other ends of the spectrum (those that receive too many items from the float, and those that lose too many) can easily dominate the conversation, drowning out the "no-drama" branches where floating is a nonissue. Some decision makers have let this imbalance scare them into choosing not to float. This is a mistake, as great benefits can be gathered from floating. When interviewing staff members from a floating system, some of whom may be negative about floating due to imbalanced collections in some branches, always ask that system's leadership this question: what percentage of branches needs to be rebalanced on a daily basis? For most systems, the answer is 20 percent or less, which means that 80 percent of the branches are doing just fine.

A few branches will receive far too many items from the float, and some branches—often including the main library—will watch their most desirable items float away, never to return. This rebalancing problem can appear deceptively simple. If some branches have too much material and other branches do not have enough, surely the "haves" can simply ship items to the "have-nots"—and, in fact, sometimes this works. But sometimes the problem is deeper than that, and for a branch as big as a main library, for example, all the extra shipping will not result in better-stocked shelves. Why? Because as the more-desirable materials float to smaller branches, patrons snap them up, resulting in increased circulation. And items in circulation cannot be on a shelf, which means that shelves are emptier all over the system, but particularly in "have-not" branches. So with all the disruption of the collection that ensues, why do systems choose to float?

THE ADVANTAGES AND DISADVANTAGES OF A FLOATING COLLECTION

It is often assumed that the only reason for floating a library collection is to save money. While floating definitely saves money, there are other excellent reasons to float. Here are 10 great reasons that dozens of public libraries have embraced floating and never looked back.

1. *Floating saves a lot of money.* Floating saves money on delivery costs, usually in direct relation to the geographic size of the systems. In a city-wide or county-wide system that covers a sprawling geographic area, floating can save a lot of money, but even for systems without big geographic challenges, floating still reduces delivery and material handling costs. Fewer trucks mean less fuel, mileage, and vehicle maintenance. If delivery is contracted out it saves on contract costs for that service.

2. *Floating pleases patrons and increases circulation,* for these reasons:

   a. Constantly refreshed collections mean better browsing, more opportunities for readers' advisory and merchandising, and increased circulation.

   b. Patrons will swear that more items are being purchased when in fact the opposite is true. Fewer copies need to be purchased because materials spend more time out of delivery trucks and more time on shelves, and because copies can land where they are most needed, making items readily available for circulation.

   c. Patrons who forget to pick up their held items in a timely fashion are *delighted* to find that the item has not shipped back to an owning branch but is instead awaiting them in their home branch collection. This reduces patron frustration as well as staff time that would have been needed to reorder the item and send it a second time.

3. *Floating saves a lot of time.* Circulation staff members love floating collections, because hours spent routing items back to their owning locations are eliminated, freeing up staff time for more important, less repetitive tasks.

4. *Floating forces improved collection management:* selection, weeding, and responsiveness to patrons' preferences and needs come to the fore when working with a floating collection. Beginning and maintaining a floating collection has many positive side effects on collection work itself.

5. *Floating saves wear and tear on staff and on items.* Fewer delivery bins to toss onto trucks equal less wear and tear ergonomically on staff members, less unnecessary handling of items, less wear and tear on the materials themselves.

6. *Floating saves paging/shelving time, providing faster customer service.* In a better-weeded, better-maintained, and more active collection, less time is spent hunting items to be sent to a patron at another branch.

7. *Floating saves a lot of money in collection budgets.* No longer does every small branch or every heavily hit branch require a copy of every title. Instead, a smaller number of items can serve to enrich many branch collections as they travel throughout the system.

8. *Floating saves time in processing materials.* Because labels are centralized and items do not have to be marked with owning location labels, processing time and costs are reduced whether done in-house or through a vendor.

9. *Buying is based on patron behavior, not staff opinion.* Floating helps to perfect collection development because patrons are participating in the process. Private industry spends millions of dollars for marketing information about customer tastes. With a floating collection, patrons make their selections as they check out materials and then *return* the choices they have made, thus giving their librarians precious information about their "buying" habits, needs, and preferences. All the staff has to do is look.

10. *Floating enriches the entire collection and helps the invisible customer become visible.* Big branches have to "share the wealth" and let their premium resources reside in the less-rarified world of busy smaller branches. Whether selection is centralized or not, floating helps librarians to recognize groups, minorities, and cultures who are using the library. These customers may have been previously ignored, consciously or not, by librarians who tend to see patrons with similar values and the cultural norms more closely aligned with their own. By pooling their selections in branches that may not have previously recognized the extent of the demand, romance readers, gay/lesbian readers, street lit readers, and others can make their voices heard, simply by making their choices visible. Floating collections are a vote for democracy in a selection system long dominated by white middle class women of a certain age, as less-mainstream collections gather in numbers too great to ignore.

Need to convince a board that floating is the next big thing? The "10 Great Reasons" list above is reproduced in Appendix A.

Why NOT Float?

The single biggest reason not to float is that floating demands a constant rebalancing act in the 10 to 20 percent of the branches that are either "heavily hit" or "have-nots." Some branches get way too much, and the main library loses a percentage of its collection. The rebalancing act is frustrating and very time consuming for staff, an unfortunate reality of floating that simply never goes away. It is also a hidden cost. Yes, floating saves a lot of money, but there is a not-insubstantial hidden labor cost in the hours spent rebalancing by staff members in these branches—emailing, packing, checking in, and constantly "taking the temperature" of the health and size of branch collections. Because this work is usually done by librarians, it is more expensive than labor costs elsewhere. Is this cost substantial enough to make floating unprofitable? Not at all. But it does need to be acknowledged, and staffing may need to be adjusted in affected branches to make the necessary rebalancing practical and effective.

WHO FLOATS, WHO DOES NOT, AND WHY
Who Floats?
Public Libraries

Most floating collections live within public library systems, ranging from those with only a main library and a single branch to library systems with dozens of branches. In some states like Ohio, it can be a challenge to find a system that does not float. As noted earlier, floating collections were once only found in geographically dispersed library systems, where delivery was a major challenge. But because floating collections provide so many other benefits, floating is now flourishing in public library systems large and small. Library systems with as few as one branch and a main library float their collections with excellent results. Here is just a sample of some libraries that have floated all or part of their collections:

States
  Arizona
  Pima County Public Library
  California
  San Jose Public Library
  San Mateo County Library

Colorado
Arapahoe Library District
Denver Public Library
Pikes Peak Library District
Florida
Collier County Public Library
Orange County Library District
Sarasota County Library System
Indiana
Indianapolis-Marion County Public Library
Maryland
Baltimore County Public Library
Michigan
Kent District Library
Monroe County Library System
Minnesota
Hennepin County Library
Missouri
Springfield-Greene County Library District
Nebraska
Omaha Public Library
Nevada
Henderson District Public Libraries
Las Vegas-Clark County Library District
Washoe County Library System
New Mexico
Albuquerque-Bernalillo County Library System
North Carolina
Charlotte Mecklenburg Library
Ohio
Akron-Summit County Public Library
Columbus Metropolitan Library
Cuyahoga County Public Library
Dayton Metro Library
Medina County District Library
Public Library of Cincinnati and Hamilton County
Stark County District Library
Toledo-Lucas County Public Library
Oregon
Multnomah County Library
Virginia
Henrico County Public Library
Prince William Public Library System

Washington
Timberland Regional Library

(For easy reference, this list is reproduced in Appendix B.)

Academic Libraries and Floating

Floating collections are most commonly associated with public libraries, but there are at least two academic libraries that float their collections. Denison University, located in Granville, Ohio, and Kenyon College, located half an hour away in Gambier, Ohio, combined their technical services functions in an effort to maximize their resources in a climate of challenging budget issues. Some technical services take place at Denison, some at Kenyon. In the 1990s, the two institutions, along with the College of Wooster and Ohio Wesleyan University, formed a shared catalog. Inspired by that success, Michael Upfold, the library system manager for the Five Colleges of Ohio, continued to explore other synergies between the two libraries. He was intrigued when he saw the floating module available in the Millennium integrated library software from Innovative Interfaces, Inc. Upfold approached Amy Badertscher, then the director of collection services at Kenyon, with an idea. What if, he asked, we floated the two collections, so that Kenyon materials borrowed by Denison students and faculty stayed at Denison, and Denison materials borrowed by Kenyon students and faculty stayed at Kenyon? Both collections would be enriched, and costs would be reduced. Badertscher agreed. The idea was then discussed with Lynn S. Cochrane, then director of libraries for Denison. Meetings with circulation unit staff members at each institution were held. After the meetings, the decision was made to designate the owning library in the "z" field of Millennium's MARC (machine readable cataloging) record. This enabled both schools to provide accurate counts of "their" holdings for statistical purposes, a serious consideration for an academic library. The decision was also made to not float serials, which simplified the process greatly. Serials were treated at each library as they had always been.

Badertscher says their customers, particularly the faculty, were very happy with the results (Badertscher, interview). The retrieval and delivery are so fast that faculty and students see no downside to a book having to be brought from the other school. It is now possible to track what students borrow and where, which has made selection and budgeting decisions sounder for both libraries. Occasionally, certain areas of either collection can accrue too many volumes. When that happens, the two library staffs simply call or email each other and arrange to do some rebalancing, but this has been a very minor problem in the Denison-Kenyon float.

Other likely candidates for floating collections in an academic library setting would be large universities with libraries in satellite campuses. Rather than constantly rerouting and delivering books back to main campus, each library could hold commonly used items where they land, as is done at Denison and Kenyon.

And Who Doesn't Float?

School Library and Media Centers

In the course of researching this book, extensive surveys were conducted to determine if any K–12 media centers shared resources in any way resembling floating, and no such cases were found. There are several reasons for this. For many public school systems, money for school library materials may be clearly designated to one community or another, making floating counter to fund-appropriation guidelines. That is, for some school libraries within a county or parish system, it would be against guidelines for materials from one town's school to float and be used in another town's school. While borrowing does not violate fund-appropriation guidelines, floating would, because it would change the owning location of the item. An additional consideration for school libraries is that often different buildings have very different populations, missions, and curriculum demands, as well as very little staff. Given those restrictions, floating may not benefit school libraries enough to outweigh the challenges of constantly rebalancing to meet academic content standards and standing assignments particular to those buildings.

HAS ANYONE EVER QUIT FLOATING?

The only library systems known to have stopped floating are ones that experimented by floating parts of the collection that were not popular enough to engender a healthy float, such as biographies or large print. Because these collections do not circulate as heavily as others, floating was relatively a nonevent and the decision was made not to carry floating to other parts of the collection. A simple but extremely important maxim is that *floating activity is directly related to circulation activity*. Lots of worry and fuss can be avoided by remembering how, for example, children's nonfiction is not affected heavily by floating, simply because it doesn't circulate as much as movies or popular fiction.

Biographies do not float a great deal in any system. Although large print circulates well in some branches, in many it tends to be picked up and returned to the owning branch since the large print audience may tend to be less peripatetic than audiences for movies, for example. All this to say, in order to judge the effectiveness of floating, "test balloon" floating needs to begin with a part of the overall collection that has meaningful circulation, such as movies or new books, in order to understand the benefits that floating can bring and to understand where collections will pool.

At the time of this writing, no library system that has wholeheartedly committed to a floating collection has reversed that decision. The gains are simply too great to consider going back to a traditional collection. As Sally Houghton of Pikes Peak Library District said, "We've been floating for over twenty years. Our staff would be up in arms if we moved away from it" (Houghton, interview).

As floating grows in popularity and moves into common practice, administrators and decision makers at library systems without floating collections owe it to themselves, their budgets, their collections, and their patrons to take a long look at the advantages and disadvantages of floating for their libraries. Although there are some common concerns that loom large, once these roadblocks are examined, planned for, and understood, floating is a relatively smooth process.

IS FLOATING RIGHT FOR YOUR LIBRARY SYSTEM?

Moving to a floating collection changes more than the operation of the collection itself. Done right, it creates a fundamental change in patrons' "user experience" of the library, with all the attendant changes and adjustments. Do not underestimate how much time, energy, and commitment a move to a floating collection will take. A system that is in the middle of an integrated library system changeover, a levy campaign, a merger with another system, or other huge operational challenge is not a good candidate for floating until the other major issues have moved toward resolution.

On the other hand, floating does indeed save money. Administrators facing serious budget issues can make an immediate impact by moving decisively to a floating collection. Staff members can feel pretty helpless in the face of bad budget news, and floating is a way for everyone to do something that will have a very positive and immediate effect on the bottom line.

Transitioning to a floating collection can be very abrupt or very well planned and thought out. Not surprisingly, those librarians whose systems have had six months or more to plan out floating and to prepare the collection experience a much smoother transition. But it is possible to float a collection overnight, by simply changing the module in the library's ILS that controls floating. A few libraries have "flipped the switch" and then simply dealt with the fallout after the fact. There is no right or wrong way to float a collection, but it does seem that a gradual transition has worked well for and been the choice of most systems.

For one thing, a more considered move to a floating collection gives more opportunity to communicate with staff members at every level. Most decision makers who have decided to float their collection have appointed a float team or committee, made up of members from computer services, collection development, technical services, and branch services, as well as representative branch staff members from many levels. Once this committee begins to meet, generally a rough timeline is laid out and work is begun to get the collection in optimal shape.

How long does it take to float a collection? In a library system with less than eight to ten branches, it could move as quickly as 60 to 90 days, if the collection is well weeded and maintained. For a larger system with ten or more branches, it can take up to six months, simply because as the branch numbers rise, the chances are lower that all parts of the collection are well weeded and maintained.

The other critical factor involved with timing is whether the entire collection is being floated or not. If only audiovisual materials or only popular fiction collections are being floated, floating can begin in a couple of weeks. More sections of the collection to float means longer the preparation time involved. The time needed to fully implement floating will also depend on how smoothly—or not—the individual stages progress.

Regardless of how small or large a library system, the initial decision making process can proceed quickly or be drawn out. An administrator who decrees that floating will begin on a particular date can set in motion an aggressive timetable, while a library system with a more horizontal decision-making field may take weeks or months to analyze and discuss whether or not to float, particularly if a board is actively involved in information gathering and discussion.

Following the initial decision-making process, key personnel need to be brought in to discuss and evaluate their particular areas of responsibility in relation to a floating collection. Some possible departments to be included are branch services, technical services, collection development, information technology, circulation, and shipping/delivery. Many such teams have elected to tackle ancillary issues such as the centralization of selection, labeling, or weeding. This is an ideal time to consider centralizing functions, but of course, doing so will add some time to the implementation process.

One of the most critical decisions to be made during this period is what parts of a collection to float. Team members have to weigh the pros and cons of floating the entire collection versus parts of it and decide how to proceed. Many float teams start with high-circulating materials such as audiovisual materials or popular fiction, then layer on other parts of the collection at a later date. Some only float popular materials, or float all the branch holdings but not main library holdings. There are as many combinations as there are floating library systems.

Once the global decisions have been made, the process for readying for the actual implementation of floating can begin. Predicting how the float will behave is a simple process using tools, metrics, and information already at hand. Since the notion of floating a collection can create a lot of trepidation, a little time spent analyzing probable outcomes can go a long way toward reassuring staff, as well as saving time during actual implementation. Some proven strategies for predicting the behavior of an upcoming float are described in Chapter Three.

And of course, before implementation can begin in earnest, a plan for communication with staff must be put together. Floating affects virtually every level of the organization, from shelvers to librarians to branch managers to administrators. Therefore, communication needs to be global and ongoing, from the point where floating changes from a possibility to a reality, all the way through implementation and on to postfloat rebalancing and collection work. Staff members will have their hands full with preparing the collection to float, so it is essential that they understand why decisions are being made, in order that the collection decisions they themselves make are congruent with the overall goals. Prior to implementation, staff members will be dealing with such collection issues as ensuring that the shelving of returned materials is caught up, maintaining a workflow to keep it that way, and making sure that older items with poor circulation are weeded so that the floating materials have some place to land.

The implementation of floating itself is the work of a day—a literal flip of the switch, or to be more technically accurate, a change in the float table in the ILS. In a matter of days, rebalancing will be become a priority as the heavily hit branches struggle under the volume of returned items. In a week or two, the have-not branches will have some empty shelves, and those staff members will also be looking for some advice. Rebalancing for the 20 percent of the branches that are out of balance is the new normal, a priority that must be incorporated into workflow following implementation. And finally, understanding how patrons engage with a floating collection as well as how to select and deselect for a floating collection becomes an important task for librarians. Overall, for most library systems, this entire journey takes from three to six months on average, although nine months to a year is not uncommon.

Chapter Two expands on the decision-making process that leaders considering a floating collection must undergo. For many, the decision is not "to float or not to float" but what parts of the collection should float and what parts should not. Intrigued? Read on!

References

Article

Cress, Ann. "The Latest Wave." *Library Journal* 129, no. 16 (2004): 48–50.

Interviews

Badertscher, Amy. In phone interview with the author. November 18, 2010.
Houghton, Sally. In email interview with the author. August 9, 2010.

CHAPTER TWO

Deciding Whether or Not to Float the Collection

Sometimes library administrators and staff members who have contemplated floating their collections stop on the brink, paralyzed by issues, questions, misconceptions, and urban myths that surround floating. Sometimes learning how a neighboring system has removed a particular obstacle only serves to cement the decision to retain a traditional collection model. ("Oh, *that* would never work for *us*!") And while these issues can seem like roadblocks, it is important to remember that librarians and administrators in every floating system have faced some version of these issues and managed to overcome them—to a degree that permits the collection not just to function, but to function better than it did in a traditional model.

What is really critical to know before deciding whether or not floating a collection would be beneficial? The decision actually comes down to decision makers' tolerance of these four outcomes that occur as a result of floating.

1. Does the library system need to save money?

2. Does the library system need to increase circulation?

3. Can the library system withstand the stress of an imbalanced collection in 10 to 20 percent of its branches, along with the attendant staff (not patron!) dissatisfaction?

4. Can the library withstand the attention—sometimes internal, sometimes external—that an improved floating collection will bring to the related internal processes such as selection, weeding, and processing?

On the surface, the first two questions seem silly, don't they? Who wouldn't want to save money or increase circulation, right? But some decision makers and some situations can tolerate the imbalance and staff discontent better than others—for some, those difficulties are a real consideration and sometimes a deal breaker. The circulation increases and money savings are not worth upsetting staff members. The fourth outcome listed above is somewhat hidden in the transition to floating but turns out to be almost universal for floating libraries.

Floating improves the patron experience and, in turn, raises expectations surrounding how the collection is selected, delivered, and evaluated. Decision makers' willingness and ability to be flexible and consider greater collection ramifications—such as centralized selection, centralized weeding, and centralized labeling and processing—is important, because those questions arise quickly following the move to a floating collection.

On the following page is a simple "Floating Risk Evaluation" which is also reproduced in Appendix C. It provides a quick take on whether or not a library system is ready to try a floating collection. Passing this quiz out to key decision makers and comparing and discussing the answers will help determine whether or not floating is right for the library system—and the reasons why and why not. This is a good way to begin discussions about floating with board members, librarians, and administrators.

If librarians and administrators can reconcile these questions, the answer of whether or not to float becomes much clearer. Once it is understood where the values and needs of the library system line up against these four outcomes of floating, the decision is actually quite straightforward. Does the need to save money and/or increase circulation outweigh the headaches of rebalancing and the push to update related operations? In many cases, one's answer to that question is directly related to the position one holds in the organization.

Administrators facing the never-ending problem of challenged budgets can usually be counted on to vote "yes" for floating. For this group, saving money and increasing circulation are the top priorities, and rebalancing the collection is a solvable side effect for librarians and collection staff. Collection librarians tend to be highly pro-float. Why? Because despite the ongoing challenge to balance the collection, the heady rush of creating a collection that is refreshed constantly, as well as the information on patron tastes and behavior provided by the float, outweigh the trouble of rebalancing a minority of the branch collections.

Librarians and other staff working in those affected branches would sing a very different tune, however, as managing a collection with chronically too

Floating Risk Evaluation

Rate the library's situation by assigning the following numbers to the four statements below.

1. Not at all   2 Somewhat   3 Definitely   4 Very much

1. The library needs to save money.

2. The library needs to improve circulation.

3. An imbalanced collection in a minority of the branches and the staff dissatisfaction connected with it would be the type of disruption the library would be prepared to handle.

4. If related questions arise about how the library handles the collection, the library would be able to tolerate discussion of its internal logistics and to consider options.

Total score _____

Scoring:

A score of 4–8 indicates either that the need for a floating collection is great, but the risks associated with it may not be worth it, or that the need is moderate, as is the risk tolerance.

A score of 9–16 indicates that the need for a floating collection is moderate to great, and the risk tolerance of the library allows for serious consideration of a change to a floating collection.

few items, or constantly weeding the fallout of having too many items can dominate the workday of librarians and staff members. These same people are also, of course, expected to help patrons at the computers, answer readers' advisory and reference questions, plan and execute programming, do community outreach, and/or lead story times. There simply are not enough hours in a day. These librarians and other staff members never see the gains from floating that their colleagues at balanced branches enjoy. Small wonder that members of this minority become vocal opponents to floating.

Floating is such a drastic change to a collection that not only does the collection itself draw closer scrutiny, but so do related operations like centralized selection, labeling, and weeding. Not coincidentally, when many library decision makers begin to scrutinize a move to a floating collection, or begin to evaluate floating after implementation, they will also make a decision to centralize these related processes for greater efficiency and oversight. Because expectations for the collections are raised—patrons are surprised and delighted and it becomes a priority to keep them that way—moving to a floating collection really calls into question a host of operational assumptions that may have made sense or been much less visible with a traditionally housed collection—such potentially weak points are laid bare to scrutiny and accountability with a change in collection practice this profound.

STEERING A MIDDLE COURSE

What is the best way to navigate between differing opinions and reactions to the possibility of floating the collection? Happily, floating is malleable enough to be a rare instance in which decision makers can render almost everyone happy—or at least less unhappy! It is critical to remember that floating is not an all-or-nothing proposition. Many library decision makers have steered a more moderate course and floated only part of their library's collection. Some libraries, for example, do not float the main library's collection. Some float only the most popular materials—movies, music, and bestselling fiction and nonfiction from all the branches and main library. Some float everything except children's or adult nonfiction.

In many ways, floating a percentage of the collection rather than the whole is a good solution, because the disadvantages of floating are somewhat ameliorated when the whole collection is not involved. Collection imbalances, and along with them, staff frustration, are lessened. It may be easier to continue with decentralized selection or other practices that have long been in place if patrons are not expecting optimal service and choices throughout the collection. The good news is that the status quo is maintained. And the bad news? The status quo is maintained.

A middle course may be a wise one depending on circumstances, but the gains that attend a floating collection will also be reduced. If only a third of the collection floats, only a third of the potential savings in materials, delivery, and labor is achieved. Patrons who shop for movies and best-sellers will be thrilled and create an increase in circulation as a result, but what about the parent of a preschooler looking for fresh picture books he or she has not seen before? Clearly, there is a lot at stake when weighing these outcomes. Another tack taken by many library decision makers is to begin by floating a part of the collection, adding portions as they go along. This very common approach is a good way to test the processes involved and identifies potential risks and roadblocks. Whatever the decision or approach, no library system lays claim to a perfectly balanced floating collection with a staff that supports it 100 percent.

HOW WILL FLOATING AFFECT THE PATRONS?

For decision makers at a public library—and most libraries with floating collections are public libraries—the central question that cannot be far from any discussion of floating is the effect on the patron experience. What becomes immediately apparent when floating begins is that floating, done well, is a nonevent for patrons. Patrons immediately perceive the change in a very positive way. They will exclaim about increased selection and ask when all the new movies were purchased! The ones that do not comment verbally "comment" by their role in increasing circulation.

In branches or in a main library experiencing a net loss, patrons will question when shelves begin to empty out, which means that prediction and preparation are absolutely critical to a floating plan. Administrators must be prepared to make positive changes in the "have-not" branches, such as replacing emptying shelf ranges with laptop areas and soft seating. Floating will absolutely change the face of the space! Turning a blind eye to that fact will devastate staff morale and may leave patrons at the have-not branches feeling unheard. If staff members are involved in the process and ready to answer patron concerns with news of upcoming positive changes, patron satisfaction will be preserved as floating "evens out" the collection throughout the branches.

The other way staff members can promote positive change in have-not branches is to encourage patrons to place holds. Often, particularly at a main library or a big branch, patrons are accustomed to books and other items reappearing on the shelves. In a have-not branch, that will simply no longer happen with floating. However, once a patron places a hold and then returns the item to that branch or the main library, the item remains there, helping to restock the shelves. Just as their brethren in the far-flung branches have been doing forever, main library and other have-not branch staff members must encourage the placing of patron holds as a part of ongoing patron service.

Another way to gauge the effect of floating on patrons is to take a hard look at how patrons perceive the library and its services *before* floating. Are they happy? Are there complaints about the lack of new materials or the wait time for items on hold? One of the many things patrons enjoy about floating is the second chance at picking up a missed hold. If a patron places a hold but fails to pick it up and that item is not on hold for another patron, the item is shelved at the current location. Patrons who are a day or two late for a hold pickup can simply walk to the shelf and retrieve the item. "Surprised and delighted" doesn't even begin to describe the patron reaction when this happens!

Patron satisfaction is one of the most compelling reasons to go to a floating collection. Floating enables the delivery of fresh titles not just daily, but hourly, as patron returns are shelved rather than rerouted. The time materials *do not* spend on delivery trucks traveling back and forth to "home" branches means that the hot materials are available faster, eliminating wait time for patrons and expanding their choices.

HOW WILL FLOATING AFFECT CIRCULATION?

Floating a collection improves circulation: sometimes dramatically—reported gains of 10 percent and over are not uncommon—sometimes more modestly, but not a single librarian in a floating collection reported a drop in circulation when floating began, nor even circulation remaining flat. Why is this? Unfortunately, no libraries have been able to collect hard and fast data that can be directly and solely attributed to floating, because there are almost always other factors involved at the time floating is initiated. For instance, because floating saves money, many library systems were converted during hard economic times. During hard economic times, library use almost always goes up. So if a library experienced an eight percent increase after converting to floating during a recession, how much of that increase was attributable to floating and how much to increased use during an economic downturn?

Other very common contributing factors include collection maintenance, weeding, and clean up. If regular, scheduled weeding is a system-wide expectation and has been regularly met, the circulation increase from a conversion to floating will be, ironically, less dramatic than that of a poorly weeded and maintained collection that has to go through a major overhaul before floating. Weeding, especially of a long-neglected collection, will increase circulation all on its own. It becomes impossible to determine what percentage of the increase can be chalked up to floating's refreshed collections and timeliness of material availability compared with what percentage is attributable to weeding.

Other conflicting factors include branch opening or closings, neighboring systems closing or moving branches, changes in branch or system leadership, and so forth. Regardless of what may be happening within the library system or outside of it, floating's dramatic effect on circulation stems from two main outcomes of floating. First and foremost, patrons are not seeing the same old collection every time they browse the stacks or new book and movie areas. Selections that previously lived at the main library and other branches suddenly appear, pulling patrons in and encouraging them to browse. The second major contributor to immediately higher circulation is that the latest, hottest materials are available upon their return and not spending time in delivery trucks. This availability is not only an instantaneous circulation gain; it is also the primary reason floating helps to save money in collection development budgets. Fewer copies are needed to meet demand if a significant portion of desirable titles are available, rather than riding around in delivery trucks.

HOW WILL FLOATING AFFECT THE STAFF?

How floating affects staff members depends a great deal on what position—and in what branch—that staff member finds him- or herself.

Circulation staff members and delivery drivers see the most immediate gains from floating. At circulation, "routing" of materials to the home branch stops the same instant that floating begins, freeing circulation staff members for more complex tasks. Delivery drivers, accordingly, see an immediate decrease in the number of bins handled. How much of a decrease in delivery is a frequently asked question that has as many answers as floating libraries. Is the entire collection floating? The greater the percentage of the collection that floats, the more dramatic the reduction of bins in delivery. If a smaller percentage of the collection floats, the reduction in bins is also smaller.

Librarians and branch staff members often have great trepidation about floating because they know their collections very well. Most who have worked in a branch for any length of time have the collection memorized, shelf by shelf. "How will we know our collection?" is a common question from librarians and branch staff members. This is a concern that dissolves immediately after floating's inception, for two reasons. First, while movies and new book sections, because of their higher circulation, will morph very quickly and frequently, collections like nonfiction and children's, with their lower circulation, will take much longer to transform. Staff may dread walking in to a completely new collection every day, but floating affects the collection much more gradually than that. When floating actually begins, staff members relax about this issue. For the majority of librarians and branch staff, floating is a very welcome change, because instead of placing holds on items held at bigger branches or the main library, they are finding those items on their shelves and handing them directly to patrons. The wealth is shared, and for the first time, their patrons are benefitting from it.

However, librarians at branches that are "heavily hit"—those branches that are inundated with returns—definitely experience floating as too much of a good thing. As noted earlier, their daily workflow now has to accommodate a serious investment of time to send extra materials to branches that need them, or to weed furiously to make room on the shelves for the items borne in relentlessly by the float. Librarians and branch staff in the have-not branches can easily become frustrated with their emptying shelves if branch managers and administrators are not poised to react quickly to the changing collection.

Whether processing is done within the library system or outsourced, it is no longer necessary to place branch-specific labels on items. For internal processing staff, this is an immediate time-saver; for those library systems that outsource labeling, money can be recouped when the vendor is asked to stop labeling items a week or two before floating begins. Frequently branch librarians and staff members will do localized labeling—adding dots, letters, colored tape, and all manner of marks and notations—usually designed to help local pages or shelvers put items in a specific place (easy first readers versus more-advanced first readers, for example). With floating, this "rogue" labeling above and beyond the library system's accepted notation and labeling system is even more of a waste of time than it would be normally. Since items float, a blue dot on a first reader that shows up at the next branch will be meaningless. It is a good idea when first talking to branch staff members about floating to end local marking and labeling then, at the outset. As noted earlier, the biggest fans of floating tend to be librarians who work with the collection in some fashion or another. Floating reveals what branches need what type and format of items. No longer do collection librarians have to rely solely on staff opinion; rather, they can combine staff opinion with the hard facts of what parts of the collection land where, as well as what parts of the collection, previously thought inviolate by local staff members, actually underperform and do not float or circulate well. Additionally, collection librarians see the positive impact of floating on the collection budget. The most immediate gain is that fewer copies of bestsellers and other hot materials need to be purchased (or leased, as the case may be).

And finally, administrators and finance staff are very positive about floating. The savings in delivery and the collection budget, less wear and tear on materials, and increased time available for circulation staff, not to mention the increase in circulation, is congruent with the library's mission and something board members and other key partners can readily understand and appreciate.

HOW WILL FLOATING AFFECT THE COLLECTION?

In the short term, the collection spreads out to meet the demands of the various communities a particular library system serves. Simply put, this is why so many main libraries have empty ranges after floating begins. If a main library is way too big for the actual immediate patrons that it serves, and most of them are, then the collection will thin out and pool at other branches where the demand for those items is heavier. Six months to a year after floating begins, errors in selection are very apparent. Most of the collection will have experienced some movement. If items are still sitting on a shelf, untouched, chances are good that they should not have been placed in that branch in the first place, and neither will they be circulating in the near future. Even though most library systems weed aggressively before floating, six months to a year in, it is a good idea to do another stringent weed to get the items out of the collection that have not succeeded in a floating environment.

Long-term collection integrity becomes an important concern for collection librarians. Core collection work, for example, usually becomes a more central function as librarians in branches have no way of knowing—or informing collection development—of replacement needs, as they cannot readily know what is floating and what is available in other branches. Over the long term, the collection looks very much the same as it always has; it simply moves faster and may be spread less evenly than it has been before.

HOW WILL FLOATING AFFECT FELLOW CONSORTIA LIBRARIES?

Floating does not affect other libraries in a consortia situation. A library that converts to floating continues to send and receive items as always. Internally, depending on how and where these functions were carried on in the past, adjustments might have to be made, but fulfillment is usually faster, as once again, items do not travel to "home" branches and are available to be pulled as soon as they are checked in.

ARE THERE OTHER MIND-BENDING, PARADIGM-SHIFTING, MAJOR UPHEAVALS TAKING PLACE?

If so, then even if floating seems the perfect way to go, it is wise to wait until levies are passed, new directors are in place, computer systems have been converted, buildings built, and other system-wide projects done. Floating is not difficult, but it is all engrossing. Trying to convert to a floating collection while doing any of the above would be less than optimal for all concerned, to say the least. Conditions do not need to be perfect to convert to a floating collection, but center stage needs to be available, because floating will definitely end up there for several weeks.

HAVE LIKE LIBRARIES CONVERTED SUCCESSFULLY TO FLOATING?

This is a great question. If there is a system similar in number of branches and in collection size, their experience converting to floating might serve as a good predictor—or a good example of what to avoid! If at all possible, an actual visit can be highly instructive, particularly to see the heavily hit branches, main library, and so forth. Seeing the reality of how a floating system functions takes some of the urban myths out of the discussion.

WHAT ARE THE HIDDEN COSTS OR RISKS?

A frequently overlooked cost to floating is the cost of rebalancing. Even if only a few branches are affected, it is very important to remember that the problem of rebalancing never goes away. There is a constant need to readjust, try new methods, and fight the good fight to make sure all the branches have enough material, but not too much. Frequently overlooked is that this rebalancing is often done by the most highly paid librarians in the branch, and they are often consulting with the more highly paid librarians in collection development and branch services, not to mention the shipping and delivery managers. Put simply: rebalancing ain't cheap, but it is necessary, and it is a permanent part of the postfloat reality.

Another often unlooked-for risk is that in order to gain the most from a floating collection, librarians responsible for selection have to take into account the needs of the entire collection. While not impossible to do in a decentralized environment, this collection-wide consideration is much easier to do with centralized selection. Floating often forces the "centralizing" conversation.

IS NOW THE RIGHT TIME TO CENTRALIZE?

In deciding whether or not it is the right time to float, decision makers have to be ready to deal with the bigger philosophical question of centralizing important functions. It is quite possible to float without centralized selection, centralized weeding, or centralized processing and labeling. But floating turns small, disparate collections into one large collection. Given that reality, decision makers who move to a floating collection without centralizing these functions face some major additional work. While the collection will behave as a whole, it will be much harder to order intelligently from the branches. It will be inefficient to weed without central oversight, and if labeling and other processing continues at branches, shelving can be a real challenge.

Centralized Selection

If centralized selection is not deemed possible, some kind of central oversight and communication must take place regarding selection for the floating collection. Some library systems have tried gathering a selection committee that meets frequently to discuss issues and redundancies. Another approach would be to divide subjects among selectors so that even if there are selectors working in each branch, those selectors are buying one subject (such as cooking, for example) for the entire system collection. The majority of floating systems have centralized their selection for the simple reason that it saves a lot of money and is more efficient. Fewer copies are needed to fulfill demand, which is something impossible to gauge from a branch perspective but perfectly clear from a system-wide one.

If selection is not centralized, it is next to impossible to capitalize on all the cost savings that floating will bring. How to convince Branches X and Y that they don't need copies of that new bestseller for their branches because copies will float in? How to divide a collection budget? The heavily hit branches are awash in great materials, literally. How will the money be distributed accordingly? With decentralized selection in a floating collection, it would be next to impossible to avoid unnecessary and wasteful duplication of selection, negating some of the most important gains floating brings with it.

Centralized Weeding

Many systems use the move to a floating collection as an opportunity to add some form of centralized weeding to the existing in-branch weeding practices. Because the individual branch collections become one big collection, a floating system demands that the collection be managed and weeded as a whole, not just in branch-sized chunks. Some degree of centralized weeding ensures that the collection as a whole is being managed well, leaving less room for branch-to-branch discrepancies in the level and quality of weeding being undertaken. Also, centralized weeding can help with rebalancing efforts, maximizing the opportunities to fine-tune each branch's collection to meet its patrons' needs.

Centralized Processing and Labeling

Floating makes central processing and labeling a must. Although almost all the systems that are currently floating had central processing on paper, many had branch staff members who continued to add flourishes of their own at the branch level, be they stamps, dates, or extra labels. In a floating system, this "rogue" processing isn't just a waste of labor hours; it's a hindrance to shelvers and to patrons alike, as items with mismatched labels move from branch to branch. As far ahead of the "float date" as possible, all processing and labeling should begin and end in technical services, so as to limit the period of mismatched labels floating from branch to branch to as short a term as possible.

WHAT IS THE WORST-CASE SCENARIO?

The worst-case scenario actually does occur in those rare instances where a library system moves to a floating collection in emergency mode. In a severe budget crisis, for example, a library system might have to go to a floating collection almost overnight in order to save money quickly. In a case like that, here is what can happen.

Because there is not time to communicate to staff members, there will be a lot of confusion about how to handle floating early on. Because there has not been time to catch up branches that are behind on shelving, hot materials will remain buried in a back room, and circulation gains will not be immediate, nor will budget savings. Because prefloat weeding was not carried out, branches will be receiving materials without extra room to shelve them and accommodate the float. One or two branches will receive far too many items, and one or two will see their shelves empty out. In short, it will be very messy, and will take several weeks to several months to straighten out. But other than some very messy and complicated collection work and some hasty communication to get to staff members, no catastrophe will ensue, just a great deal of aggravation.

WHOM TO INVOLVE

Part of the decision about whether to float is also whom to involve on the float team. In most cases, branch services and branch managers, collection librarians, circulation managers and branch circulation clerks, librarians supervising pages or shelvers, shipping and delivery managers, information technology personnel, and cataloging and technical services librarians are involved. Floating affects every level of the organization, so it is important to involve people from every aspect of the library system to address their particular issues and help with implementation.

Deciding What Parts of the Collection Should Float

Even before the decision to float has been definitively made, the discussion of how much and what parts of the collection usually begins. There are as many configurations as there are floating libraries, but here are some common scenarios:

1. The entire collection floats, except for special collections such as local history.
2. The entire collection floats, except for the research collection at the main library.
3. The entire collection floats, except for all the holdings at the main library.
4. Popular materials float, such as new fiction and nonfiction, movies, and music. The rest of the collection does not float.
5. The entire collection floats except nonfiction or children's, or both.

The permutations are endless, and no one solution is the right one for every system.

DECIDING TO FLOAT: DISCUSSION QUESTIONS

If the possibility of floating the collection is on the table, the following questions garnered from the section headings in this chapter are good starting points for discussion. This list is also available in Appendix D.

The "Floating Risk Evaluation" questions are very central and would be an excellent set of questions to begin the discussion, followed by the related questions posed in this chapter. Also, these questions can easily be converted to ask a currently floating "like library" to convey their experience—for example, "How did floating affect your staff?" and so on.

1. Does the library need to save money?

2. Does the library need to improve circulation?

3. Floating will create an imbalanced collection in a minority of the branches and create staff dissatisfaction connected with it. Is this something the library would be prepared to handle?

4. Floating creates related questions about how the library handles the collection. When those questions arise, would the library be able to tolerate discussion of its internal logistics and consider options?

5. Can the library steer a middle course and float only part of the collection? Would it be worth it?

6. How will floating affect the patrons?

7. How will floating affect circulation?

8. How will floating affect the staff?

9. How will floating affect the collection?

10. How will floating affect fellow consortia libraries?

11. Are there other mind-bending, paradigm-shifting, major upheavals taking place?

12. Have like libraries converted successfully to floating?

13. What are the hidden costs or risks?

14. Is now the right time to centralize?

15. What is the worst-case scenario?

16. Who should be involved if the decision is made to move forward?

17. Will the entire collection float? If not, what parts should not?

Moving Forward

The decision to float the collection is a big one, with plenty of ramifications for staff members at every level. Reducing the unknowns (such as which branches will be heavily hit) and preparing as much of the collection as possible ahead of time will ensure a smooth transition for all concerned. Chapter Three will explain how to predict the way floating will behave using simple metrics already at hand.

CHAPTER THREE

Prediction and Preparation

Once the decision to float has been made, two major questions surface for most float teams. First, what branches will be "heavily hit," and what branches will see a net loss in number of items? Predicting answers to these questions will help calm anxiety for staff members, as well as help the float team know where to step in once floating has begun. There are actually very easy, low-tech ways to predict how the float will behave, such as understanding how various formats circulate, comparing physical branch size and circulation within the system, analyzing the role of the patron hold shelves, evaluating weeding reports, observing branch collections before the float, measuring an immediate postfloat percentage, and mapping out location and traffic patterns in relation to the wider community.

The second question that arises very early in the process for most float teams is, what needs to be done before floating begins? The answer will vary greatly depending on the degree of collection maintenance and how stringently shelving standards have been maintained. Often there is a great difference in these factors between branches in the same system, but sometimes the problem is more universal, particularly if system-wide weeding has not been kept up. The good news is that with some thorough preparation, the entire collection can be fairly quickly brought to the point where the float will behave optimally with the fewest side effects.

BRANCH SIZE AND CIRCULATION RANK

Most branches can be described in one of the following ways, in terms of physical size and circulation:

1. Main branch or large branch with high circulation

2. Medium-sized branch with high circulation

3. Medium-sized branch with moderate to low circulation

4. Small branch with relatively high circulation for its size

5. Small branch with moderate to low circulation

This may seem obvious, but this is the first level of information—and in many ways, the most important—needed to predict the effects of floating. Librarians from yet-to-float library systems frequently express concern about the smallest branches, but in fact, unless the circulation at those branches is extremely brisk, floating is actually pretty easy for these branches. Floating activity is directly related to circulation activity, so the less circulation a branch has, the less floating will affect its collection. In the list above, "3" and "5," medium-sized branches with moderate to low circulation and small branches with moderate to low circulation, are the ones least affected by floating. They reap the rewards of new materials floating in, but they never suffer from the extremes of either too much floating out, or too much floating in and jamming the shelves.

The very easiest way to predict the effects of floating on a library system would be to take a map of the system and label each branch with one of the numbers above. For many library systems, small and medium branches with moderate circulation compose at least half of the branches. For these systems, floating will be more positive than troublesome, and decision makers can and should consider floating the entire collection for maximum benefit. Yes, some branches will be permanently over- or understocked and will need extra tending, but overall, floating will have few negative side effects in a system composed of mostly moderately circulating branches. For library systems with a majority of branches earning a "1," "2," or "4" designation per above, floating will most likely cause a major and permanent disruption in collection balance. Decision makers in those systems might want to consider floating only part of the collection, such as popular materials, to reap the benefits without causing permanent extra work required to manage the collection.

MEASURING PATRON BEHAVIOR

Unfortunately, how the float will affect particular branches may not be so obvious. Float team members will want to study each branch as they move closer to floating to make sure that surprises—and negative outcomes—are minimized. Large library systems with many branches will have greater variability in size or type of location, and unfortunately, they will also be less predictable using only general observations per above. Why? Because experience with a traditionally housed collection does not take into account all the variables that affect floating, such as commuter traffic patterns, location, circulation, high use of item holds, and so forth. While float team members may be tangentially aware of these things in terms of how they affect circulation, what is less obvious is how they interact to produce outcomes—both good and bad—in a floating collection.

It is not unusual at all for staff members, once they understand what floating is, to be very concerned that their branch will be heavily hit. Everyone seems to think that their branch is a "drop-off" branch. And while staff experience is invaluable when planning a move to a floating collection, this is one area where the float team is much better off measuring actual patron behavior, rather than going with staff opinion. The magnitude of returns from other branches is a critical predictor of floating patterns and overall impact, so it is really important to know where branches are relative to one another on this measure.

Why do circulation clerks in smaller branches swear up and down that they get lots of items from other branches? Because up to this point, they have spent a large part of their day rerouting those items, and since rerouting is such a high-touch daily activity, the reality seems larger than it really is. Because it consumes a disproportionate amount of the daily routine, it looms large in a discussion about floating. And it seems to bear out that the smaller the branch, the more vehement they are in this claim. Medium- to large-sized branches with strong circulation often have larger staffs. And in these branches, where staff members may have many hands doing the same type of work, the opinions trend too much in the *opposite* direction. These staff members are often too blasé about the potential impact of their drop-off situation, both because they are handling fewer items per staff member and because the task does not take most of the day, as it does in branches with fewer staff.

Other branches may have an inordinate number of patrons who place holds online, come in for self-pickup and maybe even self-checkout, and then return the items to that branch. As those patrons are somewhat "invisible," staff members routinely underestimate and under-report these activities. The patrons essentially wait on themselves in many ways, so again, circulation staff members tend to under-report this type of activity. Since hold shelves play a huge role in the floating conversation, underestimating patron activity at this type of branch can produce surprises—and not in a good way—when floating begins.

The float team is faced with a real dilemma. How to calm the concerns of staff members? When they say, "We're going to get hammered! We're a huge drop-off location," the float team members may question whether or not that is true but be unable to offer any hard facts or system perspective.

PREDICTING SUCCESS

There are four simple steps to make floating far more predictable, controllable, less chaotic, and more fact based for everyone involved.

1. Calculate a pre- and postfloat percentage,
2. Measure hold behavior,
3. Study location and traffic patterns, and
4. Study weeding reports.

These results can be synthesized with the float team's experience regarding building size and circulation. Once this is accomplished, a fairly accurate picture will emerge of how floating will behave. Once these findings are communicated to staff members, much of the fear of the unknown will disappear, as staff concerns can be answered with readily verifiable facts and figures that they can replicate themselves if they wish. Using the simple methods in this chapter, the float team has the ability to quickly verify or correct staff opinions with measurable data of actual patron behavior.

Running Reports and Gathering Statistics

The first step is very simple: if the library system's ILS can produce it, the float team should obtain an ILS report for the previous year showing what items circulated the most in the system, organized by item type or format. How much they have circulated does not particularly matter for purposes of float prediction. What does matter is the rank order of what formats circulated the most down to those formats and items that circulated the least.

For most systems and most branches, it will be a variation of this:

> DVDs
> New Books
> Fiction
> Books on CD
> Music CDs
> Large Print
> Children's DVDs
> Nonfiction
> Children's Picture Books
> Teen Materials

Children's Nonfiction
Magazines, Other Formats
Other Children's Formats

This helps predict which items will float most. Repeat this mantra early and often to all staff: *what circulates the most floats the most*. The float is driven by patron activity, so the more a type of item circulates, the faster and more often it will move around the library system. For most library systems, DVDs will float like crazy. So will new books, books on CD, and music CDs. Enjoying a moderate float will be fiction, large print, and children's DVDs. Significantly lower are nonfiction and children's books. Even in a branch that has a huge children's circulation, the question to ask is, do the kids' books circulate more than adult DVDs and new books? The answer is usually no, as a robust children's circulation usually correlates with high circulation for all parts of the collection. Simply put, what the float team is looking for, branch by branch, is the *rank order of circulation by type of item*. Many of the branches will have an identical list, but not all of them. Pay particular attention to branches where book circulation, especially new books or fiction for adults, is particularly heavy. These branches tend to correlate with high hold-shelf rates, which produces lots books being returned and needing a place to call home.

This reporting of format types by circulation and communicating about what it means for collections will go a long way toward quelling staff anxiety. Children's librarians in particular share an understandable and deep-seated concern about the potential effects of floating on school assignments and on series. The good news is that compared to other formats, the lower circulation of children's materials keep these collections fairly stable. This staff concern is a perfect example of one that can be quickly put to rest by communicating with staff members in a system where floating has already taken place.

CALCULATING THE PREFLOAT PERCENTAGE

Prefloat visits by the float team are critical to a successful launch. Staff members will wish to apprise the float team in person of many collection issues, convinced that there is no way float team members already understand the community, the traffic flow, and/or the collections. And in particular, collection development staff members working in a traditionally housed collection who have not visited branches on a regular basis to talk with staff members and observe will not know all the nuances that are important to know before the collection begins to float.

The instant the organization announces to staff members its intention to go to a floating collection, the float team should being scheduling branch visits. Optimally, branch visits should be scheduled when the branch manager and key staff members are present to talk about how floating will impact the branch and any special concerns they may have.

In addition to meeting with branch staff members, the float team needs to gather some important metrics during the prefloat branch visit. First is the prefloat percentage of items that travel in from other branches—this is very important in determining how the branch will be affected by floating. While the branch will also have materials float out, there is no guarantee that they'll have the exact percentage float out to even out the incoming materials.

The *postfloat* percentage, discussed in Chapter Four, is the more important measure; it is calculated on the adult fiction collection, which makes it a much more reliable statistic, and it is always lower than the percentage that was calculated prefloat. But the prefloat percentage is important as well. The prefloat percentage will illuminate which branches will be heavily hit by incoming materials once floating has begun. The prefloat percentage is most helpful in terms of rank. Once the prefloat percentage is determined for all the branches, it will become very obvious which branches really do not have much to worry about and which ones will have to be ultra-prepared in terms of weeding and shelf room to accommodate materials floating in.

Calculating the prefloat percentage is very simple. If at all possible, the float team should visit the branch first thing in the morning. In advance of the visit, they should ask the circulation staff members not to check in items on that particular morning that arrive overnight in the book drop. These overnight book-drop returns are what the float team will be count-ing, so they should be set aside. Interlibrary loans or books loaned through consortia are not relevant to this exercise and, in fact, are not relevant to floating at all. Since, by definition, they are always routed back to the owning collection, they do not stay where they are returned. In short, they do not float. Those interlibrary or consortia items can be routed by the cir-culation staff members as usual and do not need to be kept aside for this exercise.

- To begin, the float team should count the total number of returned items. For the sake of easy math, let's assume there are 100 items in that morning's book drop.
- Next the float team should separate items into two groups. One group should be items "owned" by that branch, and one group should be items that will be rerouted back to other "owning" branches within the system.
- Then the team should count those items to be rerouted. If there are 20 items, divide that by the number of total items in the book drop—in this case, 100. For this branch, the prefloat percentage would be 20 percent.

- The prefloat book-drop test will yield higher results than the more-official postfloat results, so the float team should not be overly concerned if they get a number higher than 30 percent. What matters is how the branch falls in relation to the other branches. They will not really see a 30 percent increase in items every day.

A note of caution: the calculation of the prefloat percentage of nonowned items *should be done by the float team*, rather than by branch staff—for two reasons. First, branch staff members are often tempted to overestimate results "for good measure," and second, it is important for the float team to really have a literal, hands-on grasp of what that collection looks like before the float, in order to fully understand the changes the float will bring. (Besides, it will earn the float team a lot more credibility if they are willing to do the work themselves.)

Branch staff members will protest that they get more returns for rerouting throughout the day, or after work, or that on Mondays it is a whole different ballgame, or what have you. There may be a lot more in that Monday morning's book drop, but the percentage still comes out close enough for the purposes of forming rebalancing strategies and understanding immediate impact of the float, which is all that is being studied here. And yes, it is possible that if the float team came back tomorrow and the next day and the next, they would have varied results, but this simple one-time sample has proven to be surprisingly accurate in reflecting prefloat percentages.

Results will look something like this:

Big busy branch	35%
Main branch	13%
Medium branch	16%
Little branch	8%

Again, the actual percentages are really irrelevant. What the float team needs to know is what branch will have the biggest percentage of materials float in and what branch will have the smallest percentage.

TRACKING THE INVISIBLE PATRON: FLOATING AND THE HOLD SHELF

The other measure the float team will wish to calculate during the prefloat branch visit is equally simple and easy to accomplish. There is much prefloat speculation (and sometimes, near hysteria) by branch staff members surrounding hold shelves. Otherwise logical librarians often predict that with floating, hold shelves will exponentially increase. Their reasoning goes something like this. If Branch A's copy of *Middlemarch* is taken out by a patron and returned to Branch B, the next three George Eliot enthusiasts who stroll into Branch A will experience a float-sized hole in the collection where *Middlemarch* should be and will order it in, adding three copies of *Middlemarch* to the hold shelf. What this reasoning fails to take into account is that the week before, three other patrons held three copies of *The Sun Also Rises*. They read them and returned them to Branch A, and now the next three patrons who come in looking for early Hemingway find not one, but three copies, *so none of those patrons have to place a hold.*

In other words, the hold-shelf hysteria sees the glass as half empty (what if there's no *Middlemarch*???)—when in reality, the glass remains half full (there are three *The Sun Also Rises*). This example is a long way of saying that at the end of the day, it all evens out. At any given point in time, items are fluctuating all over the collection in this fashion. That is what floating is. In some branches where, for whatever reason, there was not enough of something—romance paperbacks, perhaps—hold shelves actually get *smaller*, because patrons are now more likely to find what they want immediately available on the shelf.

There is no evidence from any of the systems we talked to indicating that floating causes hold shelves to explode. Hold shelves a year after floating are the same size as before the float, with two exceptions. Small branches whose collections have been enriched with the float have smaller hold shelves, as more patrons find what they want as they browse. At the opposite end of the spectrum are the hold shelves at a big branch, or at the main library. Often the patrons at these branches have never had to put items on hold, except for the most-desirable bestsellers. Both staff members and patrons are accustomed to simply walking to the shelves to get the item. With floating, however, this top tier of most-frequently circulated titles will "live" out in other branches in the system as well as at the main library. As patrons and staff members learn to cope with this by placing holds, the hold shelves at the main library or large branches will see an increase in holds, as patrons begin to understand that the items will not eventually return and that if they need an item, they will need to place a hold to get it back in.

The other way hold shelves increase is with a general uptick in circulation. Sometimes, when poorly weeded branches weed hard in preparation for floating, their circulation increases because selection has been narrowed and patrons can actually find what they want. Overall, floating has a very positive effect on circulation, and with increased circulation comes increased holds—a result not of floating, but of patrons finding that using the library has become easier and more attractive. This is a direct result of better weeding and of collections being refreshed from the float. As the use of the library increases, so will the percentage of holds placed. The causal relationship here is to increased circulation, not to floating.

So why look at hold shelves as predictors of float behavior? Almost every system interviewed for this book had one or two branches where the highly tech-savvy patrons call in books, swoop in to pick them up, and swoop out. Library staff members seldom engage with these patrons, particularly if they use self-pickup and self-checkout, and typically library staff members do not track what sort of items (or how many) these patrons check out. For most branches with moderate holds, hold shelf activity is a nonissue. Patrons will hold items and return them there, where the items will stay. For most branches, this is a pretty even proposition, with an equal amount of their own collections being held by patrons elsewhere as in the Eliot/ Hemingway example above. But for branches with an unusually substantial number of these "hold-shelf" patrons, the large number of holds they call in will add a lot to the floating activity that is generated within that branch. Again, the float team is really looking for outliers here and should simply count the hold shelves at each branch. If an unusually large amount of hold shelves correlates with other predictors, that branch would be one likely to be heavily hit by the float.

So far, the float team has three pieces of information to compare: general information about the branch's size and circulation, the prefloat percentage calculated from the book drop, and the number of hold shelves. An example might look like this:

Branch Name	Prefloat Percentage	Hold Shelf #	Location Info	Weeding Status
Clarkson Large size/High circulation	35%	37		
Main Library Large size/High circulation	8%	15		
Fuller Medium size/High circulation	25%	24		
Exton Medium size/Moderate circulation	12%	20		
Ridge Park Medium size/Moderate circulation	10%	15		
Greensburg Medium size/Low circulation	6%	13		

Branch Name	Prefloat Percentage	Hold Shelf #	Location Info	Weeding Status
Dover Small size/ High circulation for size	22%	28		
Carnegie Small size/Low circulation	14%	12		

In this example, Clarkson and the main library are the branches to be concerned about so far. Clarkson has a lot of returns that are not "owned" by it, as well as a lot of holds called in. And the main library is a net lender, meaning that, with floating, its stock will float away, leaving bare shelves. A template of this chart is reproduced in Appendix E.

LOCATION, LOCATION, LOCATION

One of the most amazing things about floating is just how far items really travel. For staff with whom we spoke in many systems, geography was thought to naturally divide their systems in some way, or in some cases, their service area was simply so huge that they thought it unlikely things would travel far geographically. If floating doesn't demonstrate anything else, it will point out what a peripatetic society we really are. Items will show up on the complete opposite end of the system, almost from the very first day that floating begins.

Location is the single biggest factor determining where items will land. Staff and the float team will naturally focus on metrics like book drops and hold shelves, but not many think to get out an actual (or virtual) map of the service area. It is critical to look *outside* the dynamics of the library system to the dynamics of the service area itself to really understand how the float will behave.

This is a simple exercise, but it can have important results, especially when combined with the information garnered about prefloat percentages and hold shelves. Take a map of the service area that shows the highways and major routes. Mark the major commuter routes that are highways in black, the main commuter arteries that are used heavily but are not major highways in red, and so on. Then mark the exact locations of the branches, and ask these questions:

1. *How easy is it to drive in, drop off items in the book drop, and drive out?*
   Patrons will go miles out of the way to use an easy drop-off and avoid a bad one.

2. *How close are branches to main thoroughfares (both highways and other main routes) that most people travel on their way to work and school?*

Needless to say, the closer branches are to these routes, the more attractive they are for busy people looking to drop off library materials.

3. *Can the branch be accessed from both directions?*

In other words, if the branch is located on a busy major route but it is difficult to turn in from the left lane to get to it, that branch will not be as hard hit as one that is easily accessible from both directions.

4. *Are any branches located on a busy corner?*

Gas stations are on corners for a reason. Again, patrons will go out of their way for this convenience.

5. *Are any branches in a suburb with a large workforce commuting in and out every day past the branch? Does the community grow during the day as people visit it to work there?*

Many systems find that patrons check out books over the weekend from the library local to where they live, but they return during the workday to the branch closest to their jobs.

6. *Do the branches abut another library system with less to offer than yours?*

Pay attention to the "corners" or borders of the systems; branches that neighbor systems with less to offer often have huge drop-off rates.

The branches that will reap the whirlwind are those branches on major routes with at least two different points of access and egress on two different streets. These corner locations, particularly if located on a major route, get hammered. And if they are in a heavy business area where many people work, or if they are on the way in and out of town in a heavy commuter bedroom community, chances are very high that they will receive an inordinate amount of returns.

If a branch location is a "yes" to several of the questions above, be very alert to the impact floating will have on that branch. In some heart-stopping cases, a branch will fit *all* of these criteria. It is impossible to overstate how vulnerable these branches are to being heavily hit and how much support they will need once floating begins.

Here's how the chart might look in the example:

Branch Name	Prefloat Percentage	Hold Shelf #	Location Info	Weeding Status
Clarkson Large size/High circulation	35%	37	Busy commuter route; corner location	

Branch Name	Prefloat Percentage	Hold Shelf #	Location Info	Weeding Status
Main Library Large size/High circulation	8%	15	Downtown location; little commuter traffic	
Fuller Medium size/High circulation	25%	24	Busy suburb; easy book-drop access	
Exton Medium size/Moderate circulation	12%	20	Suburb/not on main route, but borders another system	
Ridge Park Medium size/ Moderate circulation	10%	15	Medium-sized bed-room community; light daytime traffic	
Greensburg Medium size/Low circulation	6%	13	Small bedroom community; low traffic	
Dover Small size/High circulation for size	22%	28	In very busy lunchtime location surrounded by businesses	
Carnegie Small size/Low circulation	14%	12	Small community of mostly retirees	

HEED THE WEED

In addition to analyzing book drops, counting hold shelves, and studying traffic and commuter patterns, there is another much more mundane but much more reliable predictor of floating success. And this one can be done from the desktop. Put simply, well-maintained collections survive and thrive and adapt to the changes that the float brings very well. Poorly maintained collections suffer and are less flexible under the strain.

Two reports that are extremely instructive are weeding reports and last copy reports. The first is the classic weeding report, which shows what and how many items haven't moved in any given time frame. Running a report that shows any items with zero circulation in the past 18 months, arranged by branch, will provide an excellent snapshot of where the unweeded branches are. For many systems, because it serves a different mission, the main library is at the top of this list. This particular question again illustrates that in some library systems—but not all—the main library serves a very different purpose, mission, and clientele. For such library systems, it is worthwhile to discuss whether or not the majority of the main library's collection should float. And this is a good juncture to evaluate that. If a considerable portion of the main library's collection has not circulated in the past 18 months, and if that is considered acceptable under the library's overall mission, then it is probably wise to make a good portion (often the "research" portions) of the main library into a nonfloating collection. If, however, the expectation is that the main library's collection will circulate actively or be weeded, then allowing it to float will help to keep it vital in that respect.

Once the main library question is decided, the results of an overall weeding list will speak volumes about what collections are well managed, as well as what collections are not. More importantly, it may illuminate what branches or parts of the collections are likely trouble spots when floating begins. Some branches may be well weeded in every area except children's, for example. Main and other large branches may have a huge number of nonfiction titles that have not circulated but that the staff has been afraid to weed. Branch managers can use this information to target labor hours in the time allotted to clean up the collection before the float.

Here is how the sample library system looks with all of the prefloat information in place.

Branch Name	Prefloat Percentage	Hold Shelf #	Location Info	Weeding Status
Clarkson Large size/ High circulation	35%	37	Busy commuter route; corner location	Poorly weeded
Main Library Large size/ High circulation	8%	15	Downtown location; little commuter traffic	Poorly weeded
Fuller Medium size/High circulation	25%	24	Busy suburb; easy book-drop access	Well weeded
Exton Medium size/ Moderate circulation	12%	20	Suburb/not on main route, but borders another system	Moderately weeded
Ridge Park Medium size/ Moderate circulation	10%	15	Medium-sized bedroom community; light daytime traffic	Poorly weeded
Greensburg Medium size/ Low circulation	6%	13	Small bedroom community; low traffic	Moderately well weeded

Branch Name	Prefloat Percentage	Hold Shelf #	Location Info	Weeding Status
Dover Small size/High circulation for size	22%	28	In very busy lunchtime location surrounded by businesses	Very well weeded
Carnegie Small size/Low circulation	14%	12	Small community of mostly retirees	Very well weeded

It is not atypical to have a wide spectrum of poorly weeded to well-weeded branches. All this to say, the well-tended collections will have fewer items that have not circulated in 18 months; the poorly tended collections, on the other hand, will have thousands of items that have not circulated in over 18 months. A significant percentage will be "ghosts," or items that are actually missing or misplaced through being untended over time. Those branches who have eschewed weeding for one reason or another will have a more difficult time preparing their branch to absorb the shock of floating.

Having well-weeded branches is absolutely essential to a successful float, so this part of the float team's information gathering can also help determine how long it might take to get all the branches ready to float. In some library systems, regular, centralized weeding happens several times a year. For these systems, the readiness timeline will obviously be much shorter. But for most systems, the success or failure of regular weeding depends on staffing levels, as well as the priority and importance (or lack thereof) that has been communicated to branch managers and staff members about weeding.

A branch like Clarkson, in the preceding example, is often underweeded because staff members are simply too busy doing other work and waiting on patrons. These branches should be considered for extra hours in the preparation process, as it is imperative that they, more than the other branches, are extremely well weeded and ready to be impacted almost immediately by large amounts of materials arriving from the float.

It is perhaps not surprising that those staff members with the poorest weeding records are also the ones that struggle the most to flexibly adapt to a sea change like floating. If they have struggled to weed and have not been led in that direction all these years, imagine the upset to these staff members at the thought of "their" items floating away! Branch managers should be strongly encouraged to help their staff understand the necessity of parting with "their" collection, first through weeding and then through floating.

Oftentimes, smaller branches are beautifully weeded. Due to limited shelving space, these staff members have been forced to weed on a near-daily basis. In these branches, which could potentially be overrun, preparing to float is usually a simple matter. They simply do more of what they do every day. Furthermore, these "weeding-adept" staff members can provide great leadership and guidance for staff reluctant to embrace weeding as a part of their daily lives, both in preparation for the float and in coping with it.

INTERPRETING RESULTS

What does this example show? For the library system in the example, Clarkson is a branch to worry about. They have a high percentage of items that are "owned" by other branches coming in every day. They have a tech-savvy population who love to place holds, giving them a high hold-shelf count. They are very conveniently located in a heavily populated, busy area, and they have been too busy to weed. For starters, this branch needs to be weeded to make room for items to float in, but additionally, this branch needs to be considered as a major player in the group conversations about rebalancing—they will need help "offloading" a good portion of what floats in, at least weekly, if not more often.

Conversely, assuming the main library's collection is expected to circulate at a reasonable rate, administrators need to start thinking about reshaping the look and layout of the main library now, before floating even starts. Given the nature of its collection, many items will float out to branches and not return. The main branch itself only borrows eight percent of items from other branches, usually multiple copies of bestsellers, and because they are used to having a large and full collection, the hold shelves needed for their patrons to call in items are relatively small. Adding to that, their historic downtown location is lovely, but it has only lunchtime foot traffic and very little weekend business compared to the big suburban branches. When floating begins, the main branch's shelves will empty out quickly before reaching a normative state that is closer in size to the larger suburban branches. Floating will cause the main library (as well as the branches) to "right size" for its community, and for most main branches, that right size is far smaller than the prefloat layout. Most library systems would elect to have the main library as a major recipient in a rebalancing effort, so as to ease some of the "have-not" effect.

In the example below, both the Fuller branch and the Dover branch bear watching. They are both high circulating, and they have fewer shelves than their volume business calls for. The only reason they are not in crisis now is because materials are being routed out. Once the items no longer are routed out, both Fuller and Dover will have an excess of materials in very short order, and the system needs to be ready with a rebalancing solution before floating begins to avoid a crisis.

Exton, Ridge Park, Greensburg, and Carnegie will have the best of all possible worlds. They will see the advantages of floating but are not in danger of being overloaded. Exton and Ridge Park have not been weeding and will definitely need to weed and get ready for floating—and stay weeded after that—but otherwise should only experience the good aspects of being part of a floating library system.

Branch Name	Prefloat Percentage	Hold Shelf #	Location Info	Weeding Status
Clarkson Large size/ High circulation	35%	37	Busy commuter route; corner location	Poorly weeded
Main Library Large size/ High circulation	8%	15	Downtown location; little commuter traffic	Poorly weeded
Fuller Medium size/ High circulation	25%	24	Busy suburb; easy book-drop access	Well weeded
Exton Medium size/ Moderate circulation	12%	20	Suburb/not on main route, but borders another system	Moderately weeded
Ridge Park Medium size/ Moderate circulation	10%	15	Medium-sized bedroom com-munity; light daytime traffic	Poorly weeded
Greensburg Medium size/ Low circulation	6%	13	Small bedroom community; low traffic	Moderately well weeded
Dover Small size/High circulation for size	22%	28	In very busy lunchtime location surrounded by businesses	Very well weeded
Carnegie Small size/Low circulation	14%	12	Small community of mostly retirees	Very well weeded

Gathering these simple metrics—general information about size and circulation, percentage of book drop materials to be rerouted, a ranking of hold shelves, an informed picture of the traffic patterns throughout the service area, and the state of weeding in the system—will all help the float team to determine what branches will need the most help once floating has begun. This is great information to share with staff members. Bringing facts to a potentially emotional discussion is a great way of helping to manage change as the staff members' fear of the unknown meets the actual realities of where their branch might lie in the overall picture. And for those working at Clarkson or the main library or Fuller in the example, knowing that the float team is aware of potential problems and is making arrangements to deal with them is very reassuring to staff members. Conversely, when staff members predict that their branch will be the biggest drop-off location in the system, the float team can offer with certainty that actually no, Clarkson (in the example) will be the biggest drop-off, and they can explain how they have arrived at that conclusion.

Of course, there will be surprises. All the careful planning and educated guesswork aside, there will be some anomaly unforeseen that renders the best-laid plans open to the mercies and humors of floating. But the more measurements are gathered ahead of time, the more assured the float team (and consequently the entire staff) can be that the unexpected outcomes are limited, providing the system with a more predictable and smoother float.

CHAPTER FOUR

Communication: Preparing the Staff

If there is a single "secret to success" with floating, it lies in thorough and ongoing communication with staff members at every level. There are few other changes a library can undergo that will affect the daily workflow of so many. Probably the staff members least affected are those in technical and information services. Once the floating rules have been changed in the ILS, information services has little to do with floating. In technical services, catalogers certainly need to understand the concept of floating, and processing staff members need to be apprised of how floating works and why owning labels are no longer required. But members of the collection development staff and staff members at every level in branch work, from shelvers and pages to branch managers, need a thorough grounding in the concept of a floating library. Communication needs to start as early as possible and continue long after floating has begun, particularly in regard to rebalancing. But initially, communication is important because staff members need an opportunity to think through the ways in which floating will change their daily workflow, so they can plan accordingly.

STAFF MORALE

Staff morale is a serious consideration for decision makers considering floating. In library systems caught in the grip of budget downturns, staff layoffs, and/or branch closings, decision makers fear the potential impact of floating on staff morale as a reason not to float, only to find that floating actually improves morale. Why? Because staff members feel as though they are contributing to savings and to a solution. In other library systems, where the budget is stable and staff morale is high, floating can have a very negative impact on morale. Why? Because communication about floating, and particularly about rebalancing, has been neglected, leaving staff members anxious, frustrated, and fed up.

The key to keeping staff morale stable is to remember that when implementing floating, it is almost impossible to overcommunicate. The better informed the staff, the more comfortable they will be making decisions to prepare the collection for floating and help rebalance once floating has begun. The healthier the communication, the more inclined the staff members will be to report problems and help to arrive at solutions.

The float team should spend some time early in the planning stages to create a detailed communication plan so that this important process goes hand in glove with the other steps necessary to prepare for floating, rather than being treated as an afterthought. Interestingly, many of the staff concerns that arise beforehand evaporate once floating has begun, because floating is much more gradual in reality than it sounds in theory. And bear in mind that for most successfully floating systems, with the exception of main branch staff and staff in heavily impacted branches, floating is all but invisible to patrons and staff members alike. Once it is up and running, if communication is thorough and ongoing, floating has little impact on day-to-day staff morale.

Additionally, there are many staff members whose lives will be made much easier and whose morale will skyrocket with the advent of a floating collection. Circulation workers, who will never have to route a single item back to an owning branch, suddenly feel as if they have gained a new part-time employee, such is the time gained from letting checked-in items stay where they land. Processing staff members, who will no longer have to designate "owning" branches in any way on thousands and thousands of items, will likely also find their work going faster and more efficiently. When it comes to discussions of staff angst and floating, participants rarely stop to take into account floating's timesaving aspects and the resulting positive effect on various positions.

MANAGING THE CHANGE

Floating is a huge change, and the worst thing the float team can do is to pretend otherwise. Thorough preparation and ongoing communication will go a long way towards helping staff members prepare for and navigate this change, empowering them to look at their own daily workflow and make good, proactive decisions about what needs to be done. Many librarians have spent their careers building and curating an excellent collection. All of a sudden, they may no longer be selecting it, if a move to centralized selection is being considered, and "their" collection is no longer theirs but shared in common with all branches. For staff members who have literally made a career out of this work, can we really be surprised when they are upset and negative about change?

In Ann Cress's 2004 landmark *Library Journal* article on floating, she referred to William Bridges's classic, *Managing Transitions* (Cress, article). Currently in its third edition, *Managing Transitions: Making the Most of Change* (Da Capo Lifelong Books, 2009) is the perfect resource when taking staff members through the changes that come along with floating. Why? Bridges describes periods of transition (which sound and behave a lot like stages of grief). Acknowledging loss, getting used to the new concepts, and moving forward is a gross oversimplification of Bridges's book on managing the psychological effects of change, but the book and Bridges's approach do fit floating very nicely. If time permits, perusing *Managing Transitions* as background will help the float team recognize the difficulties being experienced by staff members and enable the float team to tailor their communication accordingly.

The float team needs to help staff members acknowledge their loss—in this case, that their traditionally housed collections and the comfort and familiarity they offered, are gone. Pretending that is not true is the worst thing a float team can do. It is equally important, according to Bridges, to then help staff members through the transition and into their new reality. Cress is correct; the book could have been written to describe exactly the process of communication that the float team needs to go through to help staff members make the most of the transition to floating.

A note of caution: administrators and other decision makers need to be careful not to foist the blame for predicted resistance on staff members if the issue really is their own personal qualms or lack of imagination. Floating is a paradigm-shifting, mind-bending, gut-buster of a concept, and some decision makers have as much trouble wrapping their minds around it as the most traditionally minded staff members. Be aware that a fellow decision maker who repeatedly expresses concern about staff resistance may be, in fact, projecting his or her deep-seated (and perhaps subconscious) fear of change.

STAFF CONCERNS BEFORE THE FLOAT

It behooves the float team to listen very carefully to staff concerns. As frontline staff, they know best what roadblocks to expect. Also, as the float team goes from branch to branch and meeting to meeting, common themes and concerns will arise. Answering these staff concerns in a wider forum, whether through a blog, wiki, or staff meeting, will help staff members to realize that they are not the only ones with those concerns or issues.

Here is a list of several staff concerns that arise before floating begins. These concerns and responses are reproduced in Appendix F.

1. *How will I know what is in my collection day to day if it changes all the time?*

   One of the biggest losses for staff members is the comfort of knowing precisely what is in their collection day to day. Staff members will often say, "But I have my collection memorized!" And while that certainly makes their job easier, the downside is that the patrons likely have it memorized as well, making for a very dull browsing experience. However, this loss is very real to staff members, many of whom, in the days before central selection, spent years of their careers helping to shape their branch collection. In some systems, they may still be selecting in the branch. Although this fear is probably the most deeply held, the good news is that it is also the most easily dissipated. Once floating has begun, staff members see for themselves that their entire collection does not change overnight. Because floating activity correlates directly with circulation activity, the collections for movies and pop music do indeed change overnight, and popular new books come and go at the blink of an eye. And staff members are correct. It takes hard work and dedication to keep up with those constantly refreshed collections. But adult fiction, nonfiction, and children's collections are much lower circulating, and therefore, they are more stable. For most branches, it takes months and months for a majority of those materials to float in and out. (This is an excellent example of a concern that can be quickly put to rest by inviting librarians and other staff members from a nearby floating system to answer questions—more on that below.)

2. *What if my very important local history book floats away and someone weeds it in error?*

   Many staff members' concerns focus around the perceived incompetence of their colleagues. This is most often an attitude displayed by main branch personnel toward their colleagues in the branches. Staff members at the main library will be delighted to discover once floating begins that branch personnel are as adept at identifying important, one-of-a-kind sources as they themselves are. (The float team, per the discussion below, can also choose to make some holdings not float, assuming there is a legitimate concern.) Staff members should be encouraged to bring examples of such materials to staff meetings on floating for discussion.

3. *What if patrons at my branch have cards that are too compromised to place holds? We will not get any books!*

   This is a serious concern, not just for staff members but for the float team and decision makers. After all, movement in a floating collection relies on patron activity—checkouts, drop-offs, holds, and so on. The concern is that in branches where patrons cannot or choose not to place holds, a disproportionately low amount of floating will occur. Surprisingly, this actually does not come to pass. While branches with tech-savvy patrons who place holds certainly have a higher float percentage, card-challenged branches experience the same float percentage one would expect for a non-tech-savvy branch of any kind. For all the concerns about this issue, it simply has not happened to any major degree. One explanation may be that because the staff members have a higher rate of contact with the card-challenged patrons, those patrons who do check out and return a high volume of materials are less visible to staff members, so it feels as though "all" patrons have cards with issues and avoid placing holds, while in fact, this simply is not true.

4. *I am afraid my branch collection will not be unique anymore.*

    Actually, nothing could be farther from the truth, although this is hard for staff members to understand until they actually see it take place. Because floating allows patrons to participate in collection development, customer activity brings in scores of wonderful materials that change and focus the collection more every day. Floating actually makes collections *more* unique to the needs of their particular patrons and neighborhoods, in ways the most talented collection development people in the world could not hope to duplicate. Floating makes collections more unique, not less.

5. *Lots of people drop stuff off here. We are going to be buried in materials!*

    Ah, the Myth of the Drop-Off Branch. It is interesting how passionately staff members and branch managers believe this, even when it runs completely counter to common sense. Branch managers in hard-to-reach bedroom communities with no commuter traffic will swear up and down that they are a drop-off for neighboring larger, busy branches and predict doom and gloom for floating's effect on their branch. Just as interestingly, managers in branches that are serious drop-off branches seem blithely unconcerned. (The right people never believe the Drop-Off Myths!) As previously discussed, there are simple and reliable methods to predict how, when, and where the float will hit, based on existing patron behavior, not staff opinion. Once confronted with these facts and educated about where their metrics fall within the larger picture of the other branches, branch managers and staff members may be skeptical, but at least they will know that the float team has things well in hand. Just as importantly, if there are branch managers and staff members at potentially heavily hit branches who are rather blasé about their impending status, seeing how high they are on these measures can help them to realize that they'd better be prepared for some serious work flow changes.

6. *What if there is a school assignment on giraffes and all "my" giraffe books have floated away?*

This is a common (and very deep) concern for children's librarians. As previously noted, children's nonfiction, which is of course assignment related (and therefore the cause for the concern), floats the least because it almost always circulates the least. Children's librarians are extremely anxious about this type of issue, because of course their patrons are counting on those materials being there. It helps to remind them that in most systems, the collection with the least amount of float is children's nonfiction. Once again, this fear dissipates almost immediately when floating begins, and disaster fails to strike as collections remain stable. Also, children's librarians should be encouraged to create their own "customer activity." If they know an assignment on butterflies is approaching, they can use a staff card to call in the needed books and other materials. Creating a little "man-made" float is a perfectly legitimate thing to do and is an aid to customer service. Otherwise, butterfly books can be called in for patrons individually, and the float will reverse itself, but most librarians like being ahead of the assignment curve.

7. *What if I call in books for a book discussion group and they all end up on our shelves?*

Again, it is amazing how common this question was across systems that floated. The correct answer is, "Don't worry about it." Given time, floating will correct this minor overage in the system as other patrons place holds on those volumes and float them out. It does not matter if every single copy of *Water for Elephants* ends up at one branch. But for whatever reason, this little side note to floating causes incredible anxiety for some staff members. Therefore, most systems encourage staff members to simply redistribute those books to other branches, not because it will harm the collection in any way if they stay, but to assuage the upset surrounding this issue.

PLANNING STAFF COMMUNICATION

As soon as the float team is in place, a communication timeline should be developed and communicated to all staff members, so everyone understands that more information is forthcoming and that everyone will have a chance to have his or her questions answered. Here is an ideal timeline for communication. This timeline assumes that the library system in question has some serious preparatory work to do before floating can begin. If the library system is perfectly weeded and completely, continuously caught up on shelving, then those steps in the communication timeline can obviously be skipped. This timeline is reproduced in Appendix G.

Communication Timeline

60–90 days before floating begins	**Workshop—half day for all staff to introduce floating**	Floating explained; guests from floating systems introduced for Q and A; questions and concerns answered; timeline for preparation and implementation for floating distributed.
Immediately following staff workshop	**Wiki, blog, or Q and A spot on staff intranet**	Accessible to all staff members; manned by float team; for staff Q and A and general information posting.
45–60 days before floating begins	**Branch visits**	Obtain metrics to predict floating's effect on each branch; meet with branch managers, head librarians in adult and children's areas, circulation supervisors, and the supervisor of the shelvers/pages.
45 days before floating begins	**Targeted meetings for weeding or shelving catch-up**	Department heads, branch managers, any other leadership involved in getting the branches weeded or caught up on shelving.
Floating begins!!	**Wiki, blog, Q and A spot**	Float team should be posting common concerns, questions, as well as successes reported on branch visits.
3–6 weeks after floating begins	**Postfloat branch visits**	Obtain the postfloat percentage; meet with branch managers and other key personnel to answer questions and help to problem-solve. Identify branches to be included in rebalancing work group.
6 weeks after floating begins	**Rebalancing work group**	Float team and representatives from the heavily hit and "have-not" branches.

Workshop/All Staff Meeting

Perhaps the single most important moment in any library system's communication plan is the initial moment when floating is introduced to the staff members. This meeting should be as inclusive as possible. Floating affects staff members at every level; it is not appropriate to approach communication about floating as a "train-the-trainer" kind of meeting. Instead, staff members should leave the workshop knowing who comprises the float team and why those people were chosen; that the float team has done their homework and are available for questions and concerns; that many, many other systems have floated very successfully and overcome roadblocks similar to their own; that individual branch visits will start immediately to address branch-specific concerns; and what the timeline for implementation looks like.

The float team should be comfortable answering questions with "I don't know" and "we'll find out." It is not possible to have all the answers at the initial meeting. One member on the float team should be charged with recording these questions that cannot be immediately answered. The same person should be responsible for following through to make sure each question gets answered as soon as possible and each answer preferably communicated to all staff members. When the workshop is announced, stress that questions and concerns are welcome; staff members should be able to send questions ahead of time (although they may not know enough to formulate the questions at this point) or to ask the questions from the floor.

Appendices A and B in this book can be helpful as handouts—these lists of advantages to floating and some of the other libraries that have floated can help to inform staff members and kick off the discussion. Staff members might also find it comforting to note that for most branches in most systems, floating is a nonevent. These branches are neither inundated nor deprived of materials. Patrons are thrilled with new choices of materials arriving daily, and the overall collection remains comfortingly stable.

Communication Board/Wiki/Blog/Intranet

The float team should have some kind of internal communication mechanism ready to launch the day after the workshop is concluded. The first entry can be some answers to questions that were asked during the workshop that did not have answers at the time. This communication vehicle should stay in place through the implementation process; it may also provide a communication spot for rebalancing issues once floating has begun.

BRANCH VISITS

As discussed earlier, the float team should be gathering some basic information at each branch visit to try and determine that branch's vulnerability to suffering an imbalanced collection with floating. Additionally, the float team should be doing some deep listening on these visits. Many branches house small special collections, local artifacts and books, and other items and services that simply need special attention to determine whether or not they should participate in floating. In many cases, the special collection will have long outlived its usefulness, and this may be an ideal time to deaccession it. And if these meetings can be expanded to include more staff members, so much the better. If not, branch managers should be strongly encouraged to gather issues and questions from their staff members to make sure as much as possible can be covered and solved on each branch visit. Individual branch visits from the float team, both before and after the float, go a long way toward better communication with staff members.

They also serve to allay fears that central organizers of the float may not understand the unique needs of each branch's collection.

Targeted Meetings

For most library systems, some prefloat work is needed to prepare the collection for floating. Depending on the nature of this work and its severity, some library systems may wish to have targeted meetings for the supervisors of shelvers/pages in cases where shelving needs to be caught up, or with department heads from branches if the collection needs to be deeply weeded—and most of them do. These meetings can deal very specifically with a list of "to-do items" for branches to quickly complete in preparation for floating, and members of the float team can be dispatched to help troubleshoot as these clean-up projects roll out.

Postfloat Branch Visits

The float team should wait at least three weeks before systematically visiting branches after floating begins. This is because it takes that long for floating's effects on a branch to become clear. Obviously if a branch is experiencing serious issues, then waiting is counterproductive, but for most branches, three weeks gives floating a chance to work. On these postfloat branch visits, the float team should measure the postfloat percentage (explained further in Chapter Six), observe the collection to try and spot any obvious problems, and meet with branch personnel to ensure that the float is going as smoothly as possible.

REBALANCING WORK GROUP

The rebalancing work group should not be formed until a minimum of six weeks has passed. Floating takes a few weeks to "shake out," and there may be branches that look as though they are candidates for rebalancing when in fact their collections settle down after floating has gone on for a couple of months. Be sure to invite branch managers or key personnel from both the heavily hit and have-not branches to participate in the rebalancing work group, and use the postfloat percentages that will be calculated on follow-up branch visits to determine which branches might need to be part of the conversation.

It is highly likely that the most negative and disaffected staff members, often from the main library, will be part of the have-not group, as well as from the heavily hit branches. Make sure that these critical voices are part of the rebalancing group as well. They will learn that there are no easy answers, and their issues will pale in comparison with others at the table. The members of this work group may change with time. Often, after a year of floating, branch staff will have learned, and only the truly heavily hit and have-not branches will need to continue the dialogue. Once it is down to a few branches, the meetings may be able to go virtual, exchanging information on a wiki or via email rather than needing to meet in person on a regular basis.

POSTFLOAT STAFF CONCERNS

After floating begins, the vast majority of staff members' concerns evaporate. The concerns that remain are primarily related to rebalancing:

1. *My branch is being inundated. Can't you fix floating?*

   Even though the float team has painstakingly prepared the branches that are liable to be heavily hit, it is still a shocker when the tech-savvy, easily accessible branches in busy areas are slammed. The best answer for these staff members is to ask them to help the float team with rebalancing as part of the rebalancing work group, because there is no permanent solution for imbalance.

2. *My branch (often the main library) is losing a lot of product and shelves are emptying out. Patrons are starting to notice. What do I tell them?*

   Administrators and float team members have got to be ready for this one. Talking points should be given to the main library staff members. Left to their own devices, these staff members will often attempt a clumsy explanation of floating, which only serves to irritate the patrons. Administrators need to be prepared to react very quickly when it becomes apparent that even with some rebalancing efforts, the main library and possibly other large branches are going to be permanently short of stock. In these cases, decision makers need to be ready to remove shelving ranges and put up soft seating and laptop or playtime areas and so forth, so that rather than looking neglected and forgotten, these branches look as though they have been planned for and cared for.

3. *How do I weed a floating collection?*

   Weeding a floating collection is not difficult. Staff members, especially early on in floating, are very hesitant to weed, convinced that some branch somewhere will make better use of a certain item. The truth is, floating is relentless in pointing out the nonfloaters. Because customer activity claims the worthy, anything that has not circulated needs to be weeded, just like in a nonfloating environment.

Preparation and Communication

Communication about a change as all-encompassing as floating is essential. Library decision makers and float teams who give communication short shrift run a very real risk of encountering problems that could have been avoided altogether, had staff members understood what floating was, why their administration elected to go with floating, and what to expect in terms of preparation, implementation, and potential imbalance issues. Staff morale is much more likely to remain strong if communication is open and frequent, and staff members will be much more invested in problem solving if communication is a top priority. Once the staff is prepared for floating, it is time to prepare the collection and the daily workflow of the branch. Catching up on shelving that may have fallen behind, along with weeding the collection so it can be flexible during floating, are topics covered in the next chapter.

References

Article

Cress, Ann. "The Latest Wave." *Library Journal* 129, no. 16 (2004): 48–50.

Book

Bridges, William. *Managing Transitions: Making the Most of Change.* Da Capo Lifelong Books, 2009.

CHAPTER FIVE

Preparing the Collection to Float

A common question for librarians considering floating is, "What do we have to do ahead of time to get ready for floating?" And the answer is, actually, nothing at all. All that has to be done to float a collection is to change the float rules or table in the ILS and the collection is floating. But just as with communication, there are preparations that can and should be attended to, in order to maximize the benefits gained from floating as well as to minimize the confusion and disorder that can result from floating a poorly managed collection.

There are three major ways in which a collection should be readied for floating, for maximum success. The first is to decide what, if any, parts of the collection will not float. This decision is based on some of the issues covered previously, such as how much rebalancing can be tolerated and how much money needs to be saved. Additionally, however, there may be special collections such as local history that may be made nonfloating if patrons use them consistently in only one branch for a particular reason.

The second way to ready a collection is to ensure that all returned items are shelved quickly and efficiently. Otherwise, the float can bring in all the high-circulating items in the entire collection, and they still will not increase circulation, because they are sitting in a back room. It is not unusual to have confusion in a library system over who is ultimately responsible for a branch that is chronically behind on shelving. Branch services? Collection development? The branch manager is, of course, the first line of defense in keeping a collection "caught up," assuming he or she has the right shelving supervisor in place and that person has been well trained and supervised. But if the branch manager is not making good shelving practices a priority, it is essential prefloat that the chain of command is clarified and that responsible parties at all levels are visiting back rooms and shelving staging areas in branches, to see how caught up back rooms are—or not.

The third step for preparing for floating is to weed the collections. For maximum flexibility, branch shelves should be weeded to the point where no more than 75 to 80 percent of the space on each shelf is used. For the majority of branches, this averages out to a very big weeding project, some branches looking at as much as 20 percent of the collection that needs to go. No float team has ever uttered the words, "Oh no! We've overweeded!" The trimmer the collection, the more flexible it will be, and the better able to absorb items that are floating in. Doing this collection work in the calm before the floating storm ensures that the collection and the patrons remain largely unperturbed (and, in the case of the patrons, blissfully unaware) of floating.

So what to do first? During the prefloat branch visits, the float team can take a look and help to decide what branches need help with shelving and weeding. If keeping shelving caught up and weeding regularly have not been a clear and consistent priority from the library's leadership, then chances are very good that both clean-up projects are needed before floating can begin. This is the norm, by the way.

As stated previously, one of the reasons floating increases circulation is because for the first time in a long time, the entire system's collection is caught up, with all the hot materials on the shelf, and the collection is well weeded, narrowing selection for the patrons. So rather than look upon these collection management issues as a roadblock to floating that must be overcome, the smart float teams will look at this as an excellent opportunity to focus on bedrock collection management.

WHAT SHOULD NOT FLOAT

Even if the decision is made to float the entire collection, there will probably be some small exceptions wherein patrons are better served if those items are housed in a particular branch. For many library systems, local history would fall under that definition. It is very simple to prevent a collection from floating. Those items must be in their own location code in the ILS. When the other location codes are changed to a floating status, that particular location code is not. Very simple. In other cases, a donor may have given items and specifically requested that they be housed in a particular branch. The float team should ask about collections of this type and communicate to all staff members when the final "what-will-not-float" list is decided upon.

THE HIGH COST OF BAD SHELVING PRACTICES

If daily shelving is not caught up and the back rooms are not clear, the advantage that floating brings, of quickly moving popular items around for maximum circulation, will be completely lost. After all, the goal of floating is to refresh collections and offer popular items for customers to browse. If shelvers are constantly behind, that benefit is lost. Clean back rooms and systematic, well-managed shelving is a critical component to smooth floating and to harvesting the improved circulation that awaits!

The hands-on work of preparing for a floating collection really begins in the back rooms of the branches. To prepare for the float, branch managers and the float team should take a hard look at the branch-level collection management going on (or not!) in each branch. The float team should note on the prefloat visit how many book carts and trucks are holding inventory waiting to be shelved. Are the carts dated? If not, can the shelving supervisor give an educated guess as to how long the carts have been waiting to be shelved? A member of the float team can also grab a few items from the carts and check the return dates. Branch managers who help on this exercise are often in for a nasty shock, with carts going back weeks and, yes, even months.

It is not at all unusual for shelving to be left completely in the hands of the lowest-paid, part-time staff members. While these folks may be wonderful employees, chances are excellent that they have not been trained on the urgency of getting materials returned to the shelves in order to fulfill patron expectations and increase circulation. Furthermore, it is not unusual to find that the supervisor of the shelvers is the librarian with the lowest seniority, who has been assigned this duty to gain supervisory experience. All well and good, but in very few of these cases has anyone ever taken the time to thoroughly train these supervisors, explaining why they arguably have one of the most critical jobs in the organization in terms of ensuring continued excellence in customer service and continued high circulation.

Most of their supervisory experience is gained in scheduling, call-offs, and hiring, not the reasons why the shelvers should be monitored to be as effective as possible. Branch managers often fail to see the lost circulation that their crowded back rooms represent, and as long as shelving has not slowed enough to create a crisis situation, they seldom give shelving practices a thought. Again, rare indeed is the librarian who has been trained in the urgency and potential gains to be found in rigorous inventory management.

Patrons, on the other hand, think about poor inventory management a lot, as evidenced by the "recent returns" carts shoved out to the floor by frustrated circulation staff members who are tired of answering patrons' pleas for recently returned movies and new books. Many librarians point proudly to these "recently returned" carts as evidence of their responsiveness to patrons' needs. This is tantamount to the grocery store leaving last month's lettuce in the regular produce section and dropping a box of fresh lettuce just inside the front door instead. Good customer service or poor inventory management? If collection management is being vigilantly practiced, there should never be a need for the crutch of "recently returned" trucks.

Instead, patrons should be able to trust that the most recently returned items *are on the shelf* (!!) because the library employees have made shelving hot and desirable materials a customer service priority. The circulation benefit of this is that if the patron goes to the section, not the cart, he or she is likely to pick up other items while browsing, which is also an excellent way to increase number of items per checkout. At the same time, items on the send or paging list will be reduced, saving valuable staff time, and this all in the name of getting the patrons what they want, faster.

The other hidden cost of sloppy branch-level collection management is, of course, disappointed patrons, who either must give up on getting the items they are after or else make a second trip to retrieve an item when it has finally been unearthed or brought in from another branch. And that does not take into account the time and effort the luckless library staffer has wasted in combing the back room for the elusive item. That wasted labor extends to the staff member who then has to search again for the item once it has been placed on a send or paging list. In an era of severely reduced budgets, it only makes sense to reduce the amount of labor associated with a successful transaction, and the answer is simple. If the catalog says that item is available in that branch, then it should be available in that branch— on the shelf, or on one or two carts in the back room with that day's returns.

Another principle of good inventory management that often gets ignored is that if a patron has just returned an item, it is a popular, desirable commodity. This applies not only to recently returned copies of this summer's blockbuster movie or novel, but to the books on building a martin house that are going out thanks to a recent newspaper article. If it has been checked out recently, chances are that it is much more likely to be sought after by the patrons browsing the stacks at this very moment. Every item left unshelved in the back room represents lost circulation and disappointed patrons. As noted previously, the level of floating activity directly correlates to the level of circulation activity. So all the recently returned items that are currently sitting in the back room are the very ones that, given the chance to see daylight, would be grabbed by patrons and added to the float.

And finally, in terms of floating, getting and keeping shelving caught up is absolutely critical when preparing for the float because it is difficult, if not impossible, to gauge the collection's activities, needs, or future behavior when a tenth of it is permanently paralyzed on carts in the back room.

THE 24-DOOR-TO-FLOOR SHELVING METHOD

The 24-Door-to-Floor method was developed for Cuyahoga County Public Library by this author, and its goal is the reshelving of returned materials within 24 hours of their return. It accomplishes this goal without adding a single labor hour or substantially changing the way the branch does business. It also gives an immediate boost to morale—no more cluttered back rooms to search through—and to circulation, as items are out where patrons can find them. Getting "caught up" is the first goal of 24-Door-to-Floor, but an even more important goal is creating a sustainable method that will maintain the sense of urgency and momentum. The 24-Door-to-Floor method gets materials back on the shelves and back rooms emptied, permanently. How? As the name suggests, 24 hours after a patron returns an item, that item is shelved. So if a book on baby names is checked in at 2:30 p.m. today, it is back on the shelf before 2:30 p.m. tomorrow. Like floating, 24-Door-to-Floor is an extremely simple concept. The shelving gets caught up and stays caught up. But as with floating, simple does not mean easy.

How It Works

Keeping 24-Door-to-Floor on track is easy; achieving that initial "caught-up" status can be a daunting prospect. Also similar to floating, the activity of 24-Door-to-Floor is largely determined by circulation. Most branch staff members do not need an official report to tell them what circulates the most to the least in their branch. But if there is any question, the ILS can generate a report that shows which format circulated the most down to which circulated the least during the last calendar year. For most branches, the list looks something like this, with some variation:

> DVDs
> New Books
> Fiction
> Music CDs
> Audiobooks
> Large Print
> Children's DVDs
> Nonfiction
> Children's Picture Books

Teen Materials
Children's Nonfiction
Other formats

Once this list is determined for the branch, the next step in implementing 24-Door-to-Floor is for the circulation clerks to place a dated 24-Door-to-Floor tag on each truck of returns as they fill them. The cart tags are the key to accountability in this system and will end up with much more information than just the date. Here is a sample of a 24-Door-to-Floor cart tag (also available in Appendix H).

24-Door-to-Floor Cart Tag

Date _____
    (noted by circulation clerk)

Cart shelved by _____
                    (shelver's name or initials)

Type of Cart _____
                (DVD, kids' nonfiction, new books, music CD, etc.)

Cart begun: Day _____ Time _____

Cart completed: Day _____ Time _____

Shelver's Notes:
Interruptions—meeting room set up, snow shoveling, break time, etc.

Problems encountered—800s need shelf read, out of room in audiobooks, etc.

So, for example, if the circulation clerk fills a cart with DVDs and is ready for a new empty cart, he or she would "tag" the full cart with a tag showing today's date. Some branches use a different color to indicate which date the cart was filled. Some are such 24-Door-to-Floor overachievers that that they indicate whether the cart was filled in the morning or afternoon. Regardless of the adaptations, the point is to flag the carts in some way so it is easy for shelvers to find the oldest cart and shelve it first. If they are not already doing so, circulation clerks should be "rough sorting" the returns as media, adult, and children's materials before tagging them; most circulation staff members do this as a matter of course.

One of the culture changes that 24-Door-to-Floor imposes is that, effective immediately, shelvers do not have individual sections for which they are responsible but are given daily assignments by the shelving supervisor. This is a critical component of 24-Door-to-Floor, as the skills of excellent shelvers are leveraged across all sections, not just one or two, and the liability of slow shelvers is spread equally as well. If necessary, shelvers can keep specific sections for the purposes of merchandising and shelf reading but, quite frankly, this too is inefficient. The entire collection needs to be shelved, merchandised, and read.

The shelving supervisor should be assigning this work to make the most effective use of the hours allotted to the branch. If the supervisor works the day shift, he or she should leave clear instructions for the shelvers working in the evening, and if the supervisor is not working until the late shift, he or she should leave instructions for the day shift. *Under no circumstances* should the shelvers be left without specific priorities and tasks. If the supervisor is unexpectedly out, the branch manager or librarian in charge should take over this duty, so once 24-Door-to-Floor is up and running, all branch staff members in these particular roles should be trained accordingly.

The 24-Door-to-Floor method is easy to understand because the priorities for getting caught up are the same as the priorities for keeping 24-Door-to-Floor caught up perpetually. Basically, the highest-circulating format needs to be caught up first, then the second-highest, and so on.

To get 24-Door-to-Floor started, the shelving supervisor would begin at the top of the "what-circulates-most" list with the DVDs. He or she would assign shelvers to drop whatever else they were doing and to work on DVDs until they were completely caught up. Completely. Caught up. So even in the case of a seriously backed-up back room, no shelver would touch new books, kids' books, or any other type of format until every single DVD was put away. This is the heart of 24-Door-to-Floor: stop multitasking. Hitting each section or format a little bit at a time never gets anything caught up. Also, for shelvers, an order to shelve all the DVDs as quickly as possible is a fun challenge, and most of them absolutely love finally clearing out a crowded back room space that has become a semi-permanent fixture.

One problem that can arise is that DVDs—or any of these sections that are undergoing 24-Door-to-Floor work—might have to be weeded very quickly by librarians or floor staff in order to create enough room for the shelvers to complete the work. Oftentimes, the excess inventory in the back is just allowed to accumulate, and the collection upfront normalizes to a new, larger amount of items.

This becomes really obvious if 24-Door-to-Floor happens quickly. Some branches elect to go 24-Door-to-Floor literally overnight. They close early on a Friday and have an eight-hour shelving party with many shelvers and helpers, with the idea that by Saturday morning, they will be caught up and will work at staying caught up, the second phase of 24-Door-to-Floor. It becomes very apparent very quickly that collections have become bloated when this is done overnight, and staff members should be prepared to have personnel there who can weed quickly ("ninja weeding," in common parlance), as well as personnel to withdraw and repurpose items on the spot. Otherwise, the backlog becomes items for withdrawal, rather than items for shelving. This bloating of the collection happens because the back room becomes a de facto storage room, whether on carts or not, and the collection that lives out front bloats to fill the space. It becomes easy to be lax on weeding if there is always room for another cart in the back.

Most library systems do not have the luxury of an overnight "catch-up" party for 24-Door-to-Floor. For really jam-packed back rooms, it can take four to six weeks to get completely caught up, but the shelving will get caught up, and it will stay caught up.

When DVDs are being caught up, the shelving supervisor assigns every shelver to the DVD section every day, all day, for their entire shift. If that makes for too many hands in the section at once, the supervisor can have shelvers in the back putting DVDs in carts already in order, so that other shelvers can grab them and take them out front to be integrated with the collection on the shelves as quickly as possible.

DVDs and new books are the most critical sections, so the same application of shelving hours should follow with new books until they are caught up. Once they are both caught up, the shelving supervisor then assigns the DVDs and new books as the first assignment for the first shelver to arrive on each shift. The first shelver in the morning might shovel the sidewalks and bring in the book drop and newspapers, but then he or she would immediately shelve DVDs and new books before beginning work on a send list. Shelvers coming in at midmorning or the noon hour would go directly to the DVDs and new books again, *on the same day, even though the morning shelver has caught them up.* This process would be repeated every shift, into perpetuity. Why? Because even if there are only two dozen DVDs and a dozen new books to be shelved when the 5:00 p.m. shelver walks in, they are still the highest-circulating formats. Keeping DVDs and new books at ground zero will single-handedly raise circulation. While other formats can be caught up each day after the initial 24-Door-to-Floor catch-up is accomplished, DVDs and new books should be done to completion every shift due to their high circulation, even if that means other formats go a bit longer than 24 hours. For DVDs and new books, 24 hours is actually too long and represents a great many missed opportunities.

The day after DVDs are caught up, shelvers move to fiction. Nothing else is shelved—no music, audiobooks, children's, or nonfiction—until fiction is caught up. Then, it too is added to the daily list to be "kept caught up." DVDs and new books get done each shift, fiction once a day. This sounds simple, and it is. But depending on the severity of the backlog, it can take a long time to work through catching up all the sections. Children's nonfiction might go two to three weeks before being touched. And while that sounds outrageous, it highlights the neglect the entire back room has suffered as stock has been allowed to back up. The shelving supervisor will have to hold the line when other library staff members are complaining about the wait. Once their sections have been caught up and are shelved to completion each and every day, the temporary inconvenience will be a distant memory.

The real trick is not to let the caught-up sections build back up as other sections are being worked on. The little bit that accumulates in these sections every day should be shelved every day. Eventually, when all sections are caught up, shelf reading, shifting, and merchandising can resume, but during the transition to 24-Door-to-Floor, those activities get temporarily sidelined.

Shelving Tags for 24-Door-to-Floor

The shelving tags that the circulation staff members place on each cart are an excellent way to maintain accountability. Shelving tags should be completed by the shelver. He or she notes what type of cart it is (DVD, children's nonfiction), and records the start and end time for shelving that cart. He or she should also note any interruptions and how long those interruptions take, such as helping set up a meeting room or going on break. These tags should be returned to the shelving supervisor. The shelving supervisor should take a week's worth and then a month's worth of tags, average the times, and post them on the dry erase board frequently, as in, "Great job, team! Our average children's nonfiction cart is only taking us 23 minutes! That's 6 minutes faster than last month." Or, "Congrats to Natalie who single-handedly did 27 carts of kids' picture books last month!" This kind of feedback will let shelvers know that the shelving supervisor is paying attention and, more importantly, what the norms are. If all shelvers are hitting around 23 minutes for a children's nonfiction cart, that becomes the unofficial standard, and shelvers, whether they are happy about it or not, will become cognizant of their own time in comparison.

Once 24-Door-to-Floor is in place, it is normal to have setbacks where some carts go 48 or 72 hours. Being short of shelvers, or a Memorial Day or Labor Day closing, will throw things off—for a short time. Eventually, if 24-Door-to-Floor principles are reapplied, the shelving will return to a norm of a 24-hour turnaround.

And why is this so critical to the success of floating? If a branch has no particular issues with floating—it is neither heavily hit nor a have-not branch, that branch will still see a very rapid turnaround on hot items that circulate quickly. If the normal procedure is to let those materials sit for days and weeks, the one huge uptick to floating (besides money saved) is lost, as the increase in circulation will not happen if those quickly circulating, hot items do not make it back to the shelves in short order. When the branch is among the minority of have-not branches, it is hard to be particularly sympathetic with library staff members complaining about empty shelves when the back room is full of materials waiting to be shelved. And if the branch is among the minority of heavily hit branches and the back room is full before floating even starts, woe betide them! If they think their back room is full now, they will literally run out of carts, shelves, and floor space to cram the materials that will be flooding in. But if they are completely shelved up, and they have done the required weeding to make the collection out front "lean and mean," they will have shelf space and the shelving mechanisms in place to better cope with the influx.

THE BIG WEED

In addition to having shelving completely caught up, the second critical step in preparation for floating is to weed the collection. The goal is to have *every shelf at 75 percent capacity,* in order to accommodate the influx of materials as they wash in and out with floating. Branches predicted to be heavily hit should weed closer down to 60 percent in more popular sections like DVDs, music CDs, and fiction. Those branches, including the main library, that have been predicted to lose more inventory than they gain from floating, should be careful not to weed any deeper than 75 to 80 percent on each shelf, in order to slow the emptying-out process. The emptying-out process will not stop, even if no weeding is done, and the staff members at the assumed "have-nots" need to be aware that in the popular sections, they too will need room as floating takes place. The most effective way to have the branches weeded in time is to run central weeding reports. A good start is to run a "deadwood" report, which reflects any items that have not circulated at all in the past two years as candidates for possible weeding. For many branches, this will be sufficient to create space for floating. In very poorly weeded branches, more targeted weeding reports with tighter parameters might be necessary to gain the required amount of space.

It may be that this "big weed" that transpires before floating is the first methodical, system-wide inventory since going onboard an ILS system. Many library staff members in a traditionally housed collection have been taught to weed by taking each item off the shelf; examining it for circulation, condition, currency of information, and so forth; and then either deciding to weed the item or putting it back on the shelf. However, this method falls short because it fails to compare the collection to the catalog. Missing items are never identified or eliminated, and after a few years, there are many "ghost" items in the collection that appear in the catalog but have not existed in the actual collection for years. Whether the items have been stolen, withdrawn and not marked as such, or damaged and not removed from the catalog, the online catalog still shows the branch as owning that item.

In many branches, particularly in large ones, scores of items that have been missing, damaged, and so on are never discovered and corrected, so that catalog holdings and branch holdings bear very little resemblance to one another. This situation can make the chances of finding an item for a patron a hit-or-miss proposition; it also greatly inflates the send list, with patrons placing items on hold that do not really exist. By using an actual weeding report and making missing items officially "missing" in the catalog, efficiency is increased all around. Once again, circulation will improve as patrons are finding or placing holds on items that actually exist, not the "ghosts" that show up in searches.

Shifting and the "Two Fists" Rule

It is also important to understand that prefloat collection preparedness does not begin and end with a weeding report. There must be room in each and every collection, and on each and every shelf, to absorb the float. If a weeding report garners 40 percent of nonfiction and only 5 percent of DVDs, floating will bring shelving issues immediately. Every collection needs the extra room. Further, staff members rarely weed as deeply as they ought during regular weeding periods. A clear, system-wide mandate to move items out that have not circulated in a predetermined amount of time takes the hedge factor out of the decision making for branch staffers.

For shelvers who may be helping to shift shelves after weeding, it is helpful to tell them to shift until they can put both of their fists, clenched side by side, between the end of the books and the end of the shelf. This "two-fist" rule is easily demonstrable and easy to remember, and it helps to attain a remarkably consistent 75 percent fill rate across the library system. Teaching shelvers to fit their fists between the books and the end of the shelf is an easy and fast way to get those shelves ready to support the float. Shelvers should be taught to maintain this "two-fist" space on each shelf after shelving has begun.

Weeding the Heavily Impacted Branches

It is beneficial to identify the heavily impacted branches and to work closely with these staff members to prepare for floating. These branches also need to weed more deeply than the other branches. If the average branch can get away with weeding down to 75 percent or two fists per shelf, the heavily impacted branch would be wise to weed more deeply, down to 60 percent. So instead of "two fists," the guideline for the heavily impacted branches would be to weed until every shelf is just a little over half full.

Conclusion

Preparation for weeding—both in terms of shelving best practices and weeding—can be discussed at the initial meeting on floating, and while the float team is out visiting branches, all staff members can begin this work. These tasks can and should be ongoing while the float team prepares the rest of the details for launching floating. Ironically, the worse shape the collection is in before this preparation is complete, the more circulation will improve as the hot materials are put out for patrons and as the collection is weeded, allowing the desirable items to shine through. Once this preparation is complete, the float can take place without creating serious snarls in back rooms or overflowing shelves, and the refreshed browsing that floating brings with it can be shown off to its greatest advantage.

CHAPTER SIX

Implementation and Postfloat Considerations

IMPLEMENTATION AND POSTFLOAT COMMUNICATION

Considering all the decision making, communication, prediction, and preparation preceding floating, the actual implementation of floating can seem downright anticlimactic. It is a very simple process to begin the actual float. All commercial integrated library systems, or ILSs, have a setting available that governs the behavior of an item once it is returned by a patron. Either the item is flagged to be returned to an owning location, as is the case with a traditionally housed collection, or the item is not flagged to be returned to an owning location and remains to be shelved at the branch to which it was returned, as in a floating collection. The float team should be ready on the day floating begins to take questions, whether through email, a frequently-asked-question central posting board of some kind, or a wiki where "Q and A" can take place.

Some kind of shared communication method will serve two purposes. First, it will prevent the float team from having to answer the same questions multiple times. Second, it will help staff members to see that they are not the only ones with questions or issues that need to be clarified. Usually after the first couple of days have come and gone, there simply are no questions. Floating's beginning is the big nonevent. And for the majority of branches, this relative calm will continue into perpetuity with floating.

POSTFLOAT BRANCH VISITS

Immediately following the inception of floating, the float team should schedule a generous amount of time each day to answer questions, solve problems, and celebrate successes. The more public and transparent this process can be, the faster issues will resolve themselves. Two weeks after floating is initiated, the float team needs to work quickly to engage in postfloat branch visits, starting with those branches that were predicted to be heavily hit branches. The branch managers in these locations will need assistance to reconfigure daily workflow so that weeding, repurposing, and/or rebalancing become a top daily priority. Administrators will need to understand that these branches will have less time (and energy!) to fulfill system initiatives. Then the float team should visit any other branch that is neither expected to have a net loss of inventory nor be heavily hit. And finally the float team should visit the have-not branches, where it was predicted that floating would take away more items than it returns. This situation takes a bit more time to manifest itself, so it is best to leave these visits for last. All of the postfloat branch visits should take place between two and six weeks after floating begins.

THE POSTFLOAT PERCENTAGE

One of the other primary reasons for reaching out to branches and visiting to observe the effects of the float is to figure the "postfloat percentage." This metric is an excellent indicator of how much is floating into a branch, and it must be done within the first six weeks of floating in order to get an accurate assessment. Determining the postfloat percentage is simple. Members of the float team each take a range of shelving units in the adult fiction area. Adult fiction is the best choice because it enjoys a moderate float—not constant overturn, like DVDs or new books, but not a slow turn, like nonfiction or children's materials, either. Float team members should look at each volume in turn. If an item has an owning location sticker or label from a branch other than the branch in which the float team member is standing, that volume should be turned downwards so that half the book is sticking out visibly from the shelf. All the "foreign" owning labels should be identified and turned downward on the shelf in the range. Once that has been accomplished, the books with the nonowning branch labels that are turned downward in that range should be counted, and that number recorded. Next, the number of volumes in the entire range should be counted and recorded. Finally, the number of books with "other" ownership labels should be divided by the total number of books in the range to determine the postfloat percentage.

So, if 60 books in that range bear owning labels that do not belong to that branch, and the total number of books in that shelving range is 750, the postfloat percentage for that branch would be 8 percent. This number is best understood in context with the postfloat percentages of all the branches. In the case of the fictional system referred to in Chapter Three, the postfloat percentages might look something like this:

Branch Name	Postfloat Percentage
Clarkson Large size/High circulation	17%
Main Library Large size/High circulation	3%
Fuller Medium size/High circulation	13%
Exton Medium size/Moderate circulation	7%
Ridge Park Medium size/Moderate circulation	8%
Greensburg Medium size/Low circulation	6%
Dover Small size/High circulation for size	10%
Carnegie Small size/Low circulation	5%

The branches with the highest postfloat percentages will be the heavily hit branches. Anything over 15 percent would be considered fairly high in terms of incoming materials. Conversely, branches with postfloat percentages of 5 percent and under have a possibility of being a have-not branch. The postfloat percentages are often much lower than the prefloat percentages, because using the book drop to figure the prefloat percentage means that the float team is dealing with a great many high-circulating items, such as DVDs and new books. Using numbers from the more moderately circulating fiction during the postfloat count results in a much more accurate and stable number, because fiction is in the middle in terms of how much it is affected by floating. In six weeks, the entire DVD section could have turned over dozens of times, and children's nonfiction, not at all.

Obtaining the postfloat percentage is very important for two reasons. First of all, it provides a factual, hard number to communicate to staff members. There will be staff members in branches of every size and circulation who are extremely vocal and concerned that they are heavily hit and are suffering greatly from the influx of floating. Helping them to see where their branch really falls on the postfloat percentage scale gives a more realistic picture of how their branch is actually affected. It is also reassuring to branch managers and staff members at truly heavily hit branches to see that the float team "gets it" and has hard proof that their branch is indeed slammed with too much product. Secondly, the float team should be thinking about what branches would benefit from being linked up to help one another with exchanges of materials. By the time the postfloat percentages are complete, it will be evident what heavily hit branches and what have-not branches should be at the table to discuss rebalancing solutions.

REBALANCING

About three or four days in, things will begin to get interesting for the branches that will require some kind of permanent extra attention and help to manage the imbalances caused by floating. Heavily hit branches will have an overabundance of DVDs and new books. As soon as day three or four, or a week or ten days in at the most, the float team will know for a fact if their predictions were accurate about where the most rebalancing would be needed. It is not too soon to begin rebalancing efforts at this point; the imbalance will only get worse, and it will be harder to reduce the excess if measures are not taken right away.

Every system will encounter some degree of collection imbalance. Why is this? Floating serves to normalize the size of the collection's holdings across the system, as it takes items to where they are the most in demand. If money were no object, floating would be the ideal way to tell facility planners exactly where bigger buildings and expanded parking lots should be. Conversely, the space at the main branch currently housing superfluous shelving could be transformed into more public space for the other activities for which patrons seek out libraries.

It is important to understand, and very important to communicate repeatedly to staff members, that when too much of a good thing is brought to a branch by floating, it is not because something has gone wrong with the floating process. It is because that branch simply is not big enough to meet the traffic and demands for materials in the area it serves. Similarly, because main branches were never designed to match the needs of the immediate community, but instead, the needs of the entire system, it is not surprising that the effects of normalizing the size of the collection can be catastrophic to a main library collection. An imbalanced collection is an organic artifact of floating. It happens to virtually every library system, and it cannot be stopped. Instead, the float team and the staff members at affected branches need to understand that imbalance is now a permanent part of their lives, requiring creativity and a willingness to change methodologies when necessary in order to cope with rebalancing needs long term.

THE FLOAT IS RIGHT; THE SHELVES ARE WRONG

This disparity between physical size and patron demand is true on a microscale within branch collections as well. Once floating is underway, staff members often lament the influx of a particular subject matter or format. The perception may be that too much cooking, for example, is floating in. In actuality, and this is an extremely important concept to grasp and to communicate with staff members: *the float is bringing in exactly the right amount of materials customers want and need; it is the current shelving space that is inadequate.*

The float is right; the shelf space is wrong—and this is something many library staff members and administrators just plain do not understand or appreciate. It is true of collections, and it is true of whole buildings. The float does not lie. What floating does is point out the library system's inadequacies in keeping up with shifting and growing demand. The lack of floating activity in the nonfiction stacks will quickly call into question giving nonfiction the large number of stacks it enjoys in most traditionally housed collections. Similarly, large print readership as well as large print publishing has grown steadily and rapidly for years. A library system's failure to take that growth seriously by adding more space for those collections is revealed almost at the moment floating begins.

If a system were to allow floating to work in its purest sense, there would be no rebalancing. If a library system had unlimited resources, then one could arguably enlarge collection space and redesign buildings to acknowledge the greater wisdom of the float. Since that is not a possibility, some rebalancing mechanisms must be put in to place to allow functioning space for the reality of the existing collection. Because no library system in existence has the time, inclination, resources, or, for that matter, prescience to enlarge or shrink their facilities ahead of time, floating creates collection imbalance. This is a natural consequence of customer demand on a traditionally housed collection. The most important long-term strategy a float team can devise is a well-thought-out plan for helping excess materials end up in the right place, without undermining the benefits of floating. This process is commonly called "rebalancing." The better the rebalancing plan, the less stressful the float will be.

It is safe to say that rebalancing is the part of the floating process that absorbs the most time and energy and, therefore, the most thoughtfulness and ingenuity. A note of caution: occasionally the actual need for rebalancing becomes lost in the desire to perfect the rebalancing scheme, whatever that might be. The fact of the matter is, except in the cases of gross overages (usually medium-sized, high-circulation branches being deluged), floating, given time and patience, is self-correcting. Especially in the early days of a float, staff members may have a knee-jerk reaction to the slightest imbalance. A year after floating, staff members' tolerance of minor imbalances is much greater, and the float is allowed to do what it does best: move those in-demand items around the system to where they are most needed.

To become fixated on the rebalancing program carries with it the risk of reversing the float, something to be avoided at all costs. Traditionally minded staff members have a strong desire to keep "their" collections looking as they did prefloat. An important piece of prefloat communication to these staff members is that beginning on the very first day of the float, "their" shelves will never look the same, and that is supposed to happen. Otherwise staff members can waste valuable time trying to restore their shelves to their former status, when that is never the goal. As long as staff members in charge of rebalancing are clear on two points—namely, that imbalance is normal, organic, and a desired result as it shows the health of the float; and that rebalancing should be kept to a minimum in order to avoid reversing the float—rebalancing should perform as intended.

As we discussed earlier, large branches or the main library will steadily lose a percentage of materials. This is part of the normalization process of floating and is both natural and desirable. And after nine months to a year of floating, this normalization process finds its level and becomes stable as collection size comes closer to what it should be. But in that first nine months to a year, some main branch staff members will be frantically attempting to refill their shelves through rebalancing, rather than letting their collection find its level. Staff members working with rebalancing solutions need to be aware of this. They should use every opportunity to educate and explain what sharing the collection looks like, urging patience, as eventually these collections will "shake out." Otherwise, these more traditionally minded main-branch staffers will communicate and act on perceived, not actual, rebalancing needs.

So how does a float team go about creating a rebalancing solution? The work of other systems shows a wide range of approaches. Most of those approaches operate on a simple principle: communication of an overage or shortage, followed by an action of some kind, wherein materials are sent elsewhere to meet a shortage, are weeded, or are repurposed in some way.

Email Communication

For many small- to medium-sized library systems, rebalancing is very simple. Branch staff members email one another when they have an excess or when they have a need. Some systems, to prevent constant and over-lapping emails, appoint one person per branch (often the branch manager) to be in charge of the rebalancing emails for that branch. Although simple is often best, particularly for smaller systems, it is important not to overlook two key disadvantages to this method. First, staff may be tempted to "reverse the float" and use the email method to attempt to return their sections to a prefloat state. Secondly, without some kind of central oversight, chronic collection needs may go unmet.

Take this example. A small branch, let's call it Branch A, is in an economically challenged area and historically has housed up to 20 grade equivalency diploma (GED) study guides at any one time. Other branches borrowed them, but in a traditionally housed collection they were returned after each checkout. Suppose this library system were to begin floating in a severe economic downturn. Young people are dropping out of school to work, but they want to pursue their GEDs. Now Branch A, who still has the greatest need for GED books, has had their holdings completely wiped out. The GED tutor who visits Branch A every week can never find materials to send home with his students. With an email rebalancing system, the branch manager at Branch A might be constantly emailing for help, to no avail, as those books are trapping holds all over the system. Eventually, of course, the branch manager at Branch A might email the collection development staff in frustration, but, having been asked to "trust the float," that manager may be losing precious time and turning away many dissatisfied customers.

In a rebalancing model with some degree of central oversight, collection development is aware of the increased demand immediately. It knows that Branch A is having trouble maintaining GED books and, by extension, that there is a need for more GED books system-wide. Something as simple as copying these emails to the collection development manager would place the responsibility for meeting that need back where it belongs: in collection development, rather than with busy branch managers who do not realize that their individual branch need is reflecting a system-wide demand.

Another drawback to this method is the inequity of time available to staff members. Some branches, particularly those that are heavy drop-off locations for the float and that have high circulation in their own rights, simply will not be able to find time to email their needs, no matter how desperate they may be to get materials or to send them. It is a common occurrence in a floating system that the branch staff members who have time to worry most about the smallest level of rebalancing are either staff members from very small branches with very little customer traffic, or staff members from larger branches with more staff hours to devote to such matters. The email method, while simple, has the disadvantage of being "one more thing to do" for already-overloaded staff at busy branches with minimal staff levels.

Automated or Vendor Solutions

When floating began, some vendors were offering automated solutions that figured out how many books or other items a branch needed, determined by dividing the number of linear shelf feet by the number of returns. When the ratio of returns to shelf space became imbalanced, a report would be triggered that requested a percentage of items to be moved to a different facility. The challenge with a system that looks at shelf space is that it tracks number of items, not *content* of items. In other words, a branch may be signaled to send cookbooks to another branch that is already awash in cookbooks but in desperate need of mysteries. Or a branch may send international cookbooks when slow cooker cookbooks are needed.

In the past few years, Collection HQ advertised the ability to rebalance shelves. Unfortunately, Collection HQ was designed to help poorly weeded, traditionally housed collections, not lean and mean floating collections that move quickly. Collection HQ has since been purchased by Baker and Taylor, and it remains to be seen whether or not they can make Collection HQ work well for medium to large floating library systems. Innovative Interfaces, Inc., has been working on a solution called Decision Center that also promises to address the rebalancing issue. Decision Center is still in the development stages at this writing, and again it remains to be seen whether or not an automated system can address the true "heavily hit" and "have-nots" without overmanaging the branches in the middle.

The By-the-Bin Rebalancing Method

Cuyahoga County Public Library (CCPL) faced a unique challenge when rebalancing. CCPL has no central or main library within its 28 branches. Instead, it has four large branches formerly referred to as "regionals." These branches operated essentially as a main branch divided into four parts, with various specialties (medicine, genealogy, and the like) housed in four different buildings throughout the county. So rather than having the problem of one main branch collection shrinking and normalizing, CCPL had four branches in that situation. As CCPL began to float, there was great disparity between some of the busy drop-off branches and the others in the system. CCPL developed a "By-the-Bin" method to correct the gross overages and shortages. Other library systems have developed similar systems.

The By-the-Bin method is simple. The branches hit with too much stock check in or discharge the morning book drop and process any items on hold, as usual. Then circulation staff place all the nonheld items for adults (children's items are too stable to necessitate this solution) in a delivery bin, mark it with a special "By-the-Bin" delivery tag, and route it to one of the two "have-not" big branches, who check it in immediately to change the location code to their own and shelve it. This method works well because it is simple and flexible. Used a great deal in the early days of floating, By-the-Bin has settled down to the occasional seasonal flurry during busy periods. Branches with overages now send an average of one or two bins a week, compared to daily bins early in the floating process.

One advantage to this system is that it only involves circulation staff. Librarians and other floor staff are always tempted to "keep the good stuff" and send the less-desirable items to their By-the-Bin neighbors. Circulation staffers simply want the excess materials out of their way.

A disadvantage to this system is that since the inception of floating, a few staff members in smaller branches simply throw excess materials (oftentimes ones that should be weeded) into bins and attempt to anonymously ship their problems off to larger branches. As one staffer at a bigger branch poignantly put it, "please don't send us your stuff that you're afraid to weed. If it didn't circulate in your branch, it won't circulate in ours." The best defense against this behavior is education. Once staff members really understand that bigger branches don't have any more room or any more staff time per item (a common myth), the problem usually dwindles. CCPL uses the Sierra system, put out by Innovative Interfaces, Inc., which has the advantage of showing "last patron" on an item. Occasionally when branches have continued to receive unofficial By-the-Bin deliveries, savvy circulation clerks have researched materials' "last patron" field to determine the originating branch. They alert collection development staffers, who email the branch manager with a request to have his or her staff members cease and desist. With floating and rebalancing, all staff members need to be reminded of what a negative impact this can have.

Central Posting Board or Wiki

Another solution to be used solely or in conjunction with other rebalancing approaches is the central posting board, or wiki. These are often created on the staff intranet so that all staff members know where to go to communicate their shortages and overages. This works well for large library systems, because an individual-email approach would swamp the email system. CCPL first looked at an email method but determined that with 28 branches, the volume of email, even if it went to a central clearinghouse of some kind, would be too great. Working with collection development, ITD programmers developed an electronic posting board created in Windows Access, called the "Too Much, Not Enough" board. Housed on the collection development department's website on the staff intranet, the "Too Much, Not Enough" board is very easy to use. Any staff member can fill out a short online form with his or her name, branch, email, and what it is that there is too much or not enough of. The posting appears immediately and "lives" on the board for two weeks. If another branch wants to share items or can fill the need, they click on the posting in which they are interested and are taken to an email form contacting the posting staff member directly. If, at the end of the two-week period, excess items have not been claimed, the poster is responsible for weeding them. If at the end of the two-week period a need has not been filled, a collection development staff member notes the need and diverts it to a selector's attention. The "Too Much, Not Enough" board has been very successful, in no small part because it empowers all staff to make good collection decisions and to act on them. Two years after floating, collection development continues to get spontaneous expressions of positive feedback from internal customers about the success of this method.

The drawback to this system is, like many rebalancing solutions, that it requires time and attention from staff members at the branch in order to be effective. Staff members at busy branches will still be hard pressed to find time to use a mechanism like this, but smart branch managers have corrected this problem by appointing a collection-conscious staffer to be the in-house "Too Much, Not Enough" person. Other staff members can verbally route their issues to him or her to be posted.

Send Lists

Sometimes librarians will attempt to rebalance a collection by altering the send or paging list in some way. The theory is that if a heavily hit branch is weighted to pull more materials than the other branches, it will help with rebalancing. In actuality, all this does is to negate the best benefits of floating, because more of the high-circulating DVDs and new books are pulled out, while the rest of the collection remains more-or-less untouched. Similarly, lowering the priority of a have-not branch allows it to fill up with low-circulating materials and multiple copies. There are more materials, but not good materials. At the end of the day, trying to control rebalancing with send list prioritization is like trying to shoot a bull's eye with a hundred arrows all at once. You'll hit something, but it won't be what you were aiming for.

There is no right or wrong way to rebalance, and there are as many methodologies as there are floating library systems. The float team first and foremost needs to include staff members from affected branches in the rebalancing conversation. And the administrators and decision makers must embrace the fact that some branches will need their floor plan reworked, and fairly quickly. Finally, the entire staff needs to understand that rebalancing work is a permanent artifact of floating, but the effectiveness of any given solution may wear off with time. Being flexible and willing to reevaluate solutions as time goes on is key to coping effectively with the rebalancing issue.

CHAPTER SEVEN

Managing a Floating Collection in the Long Term

For administrators and branch staff members, once floating is launched and rebalancing issues for the affected branches have begun to be addressed, floating collections become part of the normal workflow rather than the focus of intense scrutiny and planning. But for those responsible for collection development and management, the challenges are just beginning. A floating collection requires collection management staff members to look at the collection with fresh eyes. What works for a traditional collection will most emphatically *not* work for a floating collection, which is one reason why centralized selection and centralized weeding are often recommended. Selecting for a floating collection is significantly different from selecting for a traditionally housed collection. Because materials are more immediately available, fewer copies are needed to meet demand. Also, as patron activity reshapes the collection by placing different types of materials where they are most wanted, selectors must redefine what is selected for each branch.

Hand in hand with selection issues are issues of budget. Many systems tie a certain collection amount to each branch. Clearly, with a floating collection such a system is unworkable, and selectors must begin to think of the budget and the collection as a whole. The increase in circulation that floating brings means that collections are constantly refreshed, literally giving more bang for the collection buck, and smart selectors can begin to think of other ways to increase circulation and meet (or beat) demand, using the money realized. Branch visits will help selectors sharpen their approach and make decision making less random when it comes to maximizing the collection budget.

Weeding the floating collection is a huge concern for collection management and branch staff members. In some ways, weeding decisions are no different than they ever were. The item has either outlived its usefulness, or it has not. But the context becomes very different. Instead of making decisions for one branch and one community, staff members doing weeding are making decisions for all. There are several good approaches to consider when weeding a floating collection. Along with weeding, collection management librarians face the quandary of collection integrity—that is, how to maintain a well-balanced collection—in a fast-moving floating collection. Most importantly, librarians must think about how to ensure core collection items are maintained carefully so as to be always available.

And finally, floating has a huge impact on the user's experience of a collection. Collection management librarians need to pay attention to how patrons are using the collection, as well as how the patron experience can be further enhanced.

SELECTING AND BUDGETING FOR A FLOATING COLLECTION

First of all, the vocabulary changes with a floating collection. Instead of selecting for a branch, selectors are choosing items to be *started* at a particular branch. If a branch is strong in inspirational fiction, every Tracie Peterson novel purchased should be "started" at that branch. The location code is assigned for that branch, and when the book is in and ready to go, it is delivered to that branch. The chances of that book meeting its particular audience are much higher there than they would be in a branch with lesser inspirational fiction interest. The float is telling selectors where these particular items are popular, and selectors are foolish not to take advantage of that. Floating turns the conversation on its head: rather than "branch profiles," selectors now have profiles for Westerns, mysteries, slow cooker cookbooks, and yoga. On each profile is the location where the item is most popular and stands the best chance of circulating. If selectors previously would have put a slow cooker cookbook in each branch, or in most branches, "just in case," now they place it just in the specific branches that show an interest in that subject, because patrons can always call the item to their branch. Floating eliminates the need for "just in case," which provides a huge savings of collection dollars.

A few library systems distribute their items randomly in a floating collection, but that approach is a slippery slope. Items that "start" at the wrong branch will waste away on the shelf. There was an assumption a few years ago that because patrons place holds and move the items, there is no need to carefully plan where items should begin their lives in the collection. That is simply not true. What *is* true is that the higher the circulation of a branch (or of a collection within a branch), the greater the "centrifugal force" on that item. So if history is not popular in Branch A, and the newest book on Eisenhower ends up there, it might circulate, but it will not circulate as briskly or float as far as it would had it been placed in Branch B, where American history is hot.

The only exception to this rule is the highly desirable "hot" or popular items. Books, music, and movies that are popular everywhere can indeed be flung somewhat randomly out to the float, and they will travel, although allocation is a huge issue, as we will see below. Take a sample of 100 titles carefully placed and compare them to 100 titles randomly flung. The results are very convincing. By choosing the best starting place, selectors ensure much higher circulation and much better bang for the collection buck. Give items to the most appreciative audience possible, and the patrons will reward that careful placement with higher circulation.

Floating acts like a centrifugal force on the collection, and this means that sticking to old buying patterns is not a good move. The branches that are being heavily hit with material will drown if old buying patterns remain, and the branches that are losing product will lose circulation if the buyers fail to "stack the deck" in their favor. So, how to level the playing field? Leveling things out is not as hard as it sounds, except that buyers have to trust the float to distribute materials fairly evenly, and that is sometimes a hard leap to make, especially at first.

As stated above, floating acts as a centrifugal force: the higher a branch's circulation, the farther that branch will fling materials. Assume that a high-circulating branch in the system also has a fairly heavy return ratio. This branch needs a greater percentage of the overall allotment of new hot bestsellers, but they can also count on some good, steady returns on those items. They do not need the highest allotment of materials. If, however, the high-circulating branch for whatever reason does not have a good return ratio, as is often the case with main libraries, it will soon become a have-not branch. No matter how many copies of new materials the buyers pump in, those copies are returned somewhere else. These branches should have the highest allotment of new materials, with frequent refreshers of hot materials whenever the budget allows.

Do not worry about being "fair" and giving each branch the same number of hot titles. The float is not fair! Poor return areas and traffic patterns are not fair. Life is not fair. The job of collection development librarians is to try and even out the unfairness of the have-not branches as much as possible by buying very heavily for them up front. This takes some experimentation, but over a few months, collection development staff members get better at giving each branch how many bestseller copies they need, no matter how many or how few that branch might have gotten in the past.

And where will buyers find those extra copies for the "have-nots"? Not surprisingly, the heavily hit branches. *The high-circulating, medium-sized branches that cannot absorb the returns at their locations do not need any hot sellers ordered for them at all, unless the library system has some kind of express, super-hot collection.* This is possibly the greatest act of faith in the entire process of restructuring buying for a floating collection, but it is true, and it works. The patrons who call in heavy amounts of popular titles ensure that those make it to these heavy-hit branches, and in an amazingly short amount of time. If selectors insist on sending copies because the branch is so busy, they will totally overload the branch with multiple copies it does not need. Multiple copies will happen to this type of branch anyway. Selectors should be careful not to add to the problem.

High-circulating branches can also receive copies from the small, bedroom-community branches with low circulation. These low-circulating branches need a few copies when the hot titles come out, but floating almost universally sees these copies returned to the highest-circulating and heavily hit branches mentioned above. These smaller branches also tend to have customers call in a lot of materials that stay there, which is another way of saying the float takes care of allocating to these smaller branches. These branches probably do not get a lot of copies to start with. Believe it or not, with floating, they can do with even fewer, and it works.

Selecting becomes a pyramid. The highest-circulating branches with a poor return ratio (the "have-nots") get the highest number of copies. The highest-circulating branches with a good return ratio get the next highest number of copies. The small branches get a small to medium allotment, going from the highest-circulating small branch to the lowest. The heavily hit branches do not get any, unless it is for an express collection of some kind. In a week, they will have four copies to everyone else's one copy. That is the beauty of floating, but sticking to old buying patterns will make a mess of it all around, so be prepared to experiment.

Budgeting for a floating collection can be quite a paradigm shift for collection development staff members. Many systems have historically assigned a dollar figure for each branch, even after selection was centralized. This simply does not work in a floating collection. Instead of thinking of dollars per branch, the collection development manager needs to start thinking of dollars per format, age level, and subject matter. This is really a very liberating way to think of collection budgeting, and it drives right back to collection philosophy. Where should the dollars be spent? What is the priority? What circulates most? Is there an opportunity cost?

For example, because of working branch-by-branch, has some format—such as large print or children's DVDs—been chronically shorted of funds, and therefore, circulated less? Can circulation be boosted by allocating more money to formats that are more popular? Floating will show in a hurry what patrons want more of, so, in the first year of floating, if it is possible to be somewhat flexible with moving funds around a bit, that would be ideal. Collection development managers should be prepared to allocate dollars to fiction, nonfiction, movies, children's, and adult materials, and then selectors should be allowed to buy *what they need of each title, rather than for each branch*. It is actually not as hard as it sounds. Most selectors overbuy at first, not believing if they needed 100 copies of the last John Grisham title that, thanks to floating, they will not need quite that many of the next. More than that, they find it hard to believe that the busiest branches, if they have decent returns and drop-offs, will not need as many copies as they did prefloating. But that is indeed what experience and a little practice will show.

THE IMPORTANCE OF BRANCH VISITS FOR SELECTORS

Collection development librarians must also cultivate a mental picture of the entire collection. Since it is no longer possible to observe and make evaluations of a static collection as in the prefloat days, collection development librarians must be able to envision a good generalized picture of the collection. When were test guides last replaced? How are classics looking? Is summer reading ready to go? Such questions are much harder to answer with a floating collection, which is one of the reasons centralized selection is so ideal for floating. The library system needs people who think about the collection all day, every day. What branch needs more medical texts? If Branch A has too many, chances are good the collection development people know who can use more over at Branch B. So for everything from rebalancing to replacements, the system becomes very reliant on that group of people who have a grasp on the collection as a whole.

Collection development librarians should be prepared to make postfloat branch visits an ongoing part of the work week; there is no substitute, particularly in the first year or two of floating, for being up close and personal with the collection. Branch visits, even short pop-in tours, are the only way in a fast-moving floating collection to know what is going out in the collection, what is underserved, and what branches need help with what.

Also, some staff members, particularly those who work at a main library or large branch, will consistently report "shortages" of certain materials. Collection development staff members need to ascertain whether those shortages are really shortages system-wide ("we have no asthma books anywhere") or whether they are a perceived need of one branch ("we used to have asthma books at my branch and now we do not, and I am not happy about it"). Failure to evaluate such situations correctly will lead to unbalanced buying in whatever areas the staff members at the formerly enriched branches are the most uncomfortable with losing. Most staff members in the formerly enriched branches eventually become comfortable with calling in items for their patrons, just as their colleagues in smaller branches have always done. Some will not; some staff members can never let go of the glory days of their enriched branches, and collection development librarians need to understand and be prepared to evaluate the real-versus-perceived need.

A very low-tech but successful way to help staff members in a have-not branch and the collection development staff is to suggest that the branch staff members keep a list of titles for which patrons are looking. Each title should be marked as "not in branch" versus "not in collection." A simple legal pad, the pages of which are sent in once a month, works just fine. If there are certain subject areas that are getting asked for repeatedly (GED test guides in certain branches leap to mind), collection development librarians can arrange for regular shipments of those types of items to those branches. A quarterly refresher of popular first readers, GED guides, and/or yoga DVDs, for example, will help these branches as well as the greater collection. The list-making helps branch staff members to see that, indeed, there are plenty of asthma books in the collection—but at the same time, it can illustrate for collection development staff a chronic need at that particular branch that might indicate a greater need.

Another fabulous way to ensure that collection development staff members really understand the branch needs is to have them work in branches a minimum of one shift per month. Floating constantly pushes selectors to buy less of what does not move and more of what does. Time spent working at a circulation desk or information/reference desk gives selectors immediate visual feedback about what not to buy. Nonfiction DVD collections that have not moved or untouched reference tomes are good sources of revenue the next time around to be invested in something that will move. Time spent working at a desk in a branch can also reassure selectors that they are on the right track during the intimidating first few months of buying for a floating collection. This practice also helps branch staff members get to know collection development librarians, which is great for communication. It also helps collection development librarians get a working knowledge of the collection, and last but not least, it is great for staff morale to see "administration" staff members out in the branches. There is no substitute for frequent branch visits or working in branches, yet very few collection development staffs actually do this on a regular basis. These fabulous best practices result in better collections, better-served patrons, and higher circulation; they also give an excellent view of how floating is affecting individual branches.

As selectors visit branches and/or work shifts, they should be compiling copious notes, for several reasons. First, even the youngest selectors with the best memories will find that one shelf of mysteries starts to look like any other after several branch visits. Second, selectors will want and need their original good notes from the first postfloat visit to compare with the second postfloat visit some months later. Was that increase in paranormal romances for Branch A a trend or a blip? It is easier to tell if selectors take good notes. Additionally, branch staff members will sometimes demand a change of some kind in selection, such as a reduction in large print, for example. When selectors act on that information and then return for a later visit, the same staff members will then complain that selectors are under-buying large print! Good notes that are sent to all pertinent personnel following a branch visit help to forestall any confusion, and they help jog memories about who requested what. Finally, good notes ensure good follow-up. Floating can make collections feel and seem rather chaotic in the first few months. Responsive collection development personnel who can act on items promptly help both the external patrons and the internal patrons as the collections adjust themselves to the float. If busy branch personnel have taken the time to meet with collection staff, it is incumbent upon that staff to follow up and give the best possible internal customer service.

Ultimately, collection development librarians will want to use these branch visits to build profiles of each branch and profiles of areas where selectors need to collect more deeply, be that home repair, jazz, or traditional British mysteries. Selectors and branch staff members alike have to be prepared to park their preconceived notions at the door, as sometimes what has been long cherished as a useful profile for a particular community is revealed to be almost completely irrelevant, when floating shows what is really needed where.

The single biggest indicator of an upcoming "reality check" for a branch is an economic one. If a service area has experienced a downturn in its economic outlook, travel and decorating books will languish while do-it-yourself and canning books are in greater demand. Floating will point out these differences very quickly as patrons readjust the collection to serve their immediate needs, not what their needs were three to five years ago when the profiles were last updated. In the majority of cases, branch staff members who spend their days helping these patrons will welcome floating's "correction of the collection" with approbation, because it dovetails with what they know to be their patrons' daily reality. As the collection assumes a new relevance through floating (and the subsequently altered selection profiles), the jobs of the branch staff members are made easier and their patrons better served.

As we have seen here, the selectors' role is recast by floating. First and foremost, selectors should be out in the branches, gathering information from the float and using that information to select more strategically. Selectors and other collection development personnel also must keep an eye on the overall integrity of the collection, which can be challenging in a floating collection. Collection development librarians should not be afraid to take the lead in weeding efforts, as this can be daunting for branch staff members, especially in the early days of floating. Selectors also need to be proactive and fearless when it comes to distributing and allocating items. Failure to snap out of the old ways can wreak havoc quickly on a floating collection.

FLOATING AND CIRCULATION

Hard numbers showing the effect of floating on circulation are very hard to come by, for the obvious reason that floating does not exist in a vacuum. In many cases, library systems begin to float in the face of economic challenges. At the same time, patrons use the library more because of the overall down economy. Similarly, a building program, or a levy that passes and brings more collection money, patron visits, and programming can all create additional reasons why circulation increases. In systems with historically poor collection management, a library system will see a circulation increase with floating simply because of the attention the collection is being paid in preparation. Shelving is caught up, and, more importantly, the entire collection is thoroughly weeded, sometimes for the first time. Those changes alone would raise circulation. It is in interesting to note, though, that no floating library has ever reported a loss in circulation due to floating. Every system registers some kind of increase, above and beyond what would be normally expected due to other concurrent factors.

The single biggest reason floating increases circulation is that items no longer spend hours and days riding around on trucks. Patron A returns a hot book and Patron B grabs it five minutes later, because the hot item is no longer rerouted to an owning branch. This is also one of the main reasons that floating saves money for collection budgets. If circulation is up, it seems counterintuitive that fewer copies of bestsellers need to be purchased, but that is the case, and it is a dramatic effect of floating. But consider this. The hottest books would go out the most and also garner the most holds. Therefore, the hottest books travelled the most and spent the most time on a delivery truck.

That quick improvement in user experience has long-term consequences. Patrons are seeing their holds satisfied more quickly, and in turn, they are placing more holds, because their belief is reinforced that the library will come through in time with what they need. Over a year or so the long-term increase in circulation and patron satisfaction becomes a permanent side effect of a floating collection. When the need to reroute these items back to an owning location goes away with floating, the result is an exponential increase in patrons' ability to grab and check out those items. Circulation goes up, but fewer actual copies are needed to fill holds. Again, one of the immediate gains of floating is that hot titles stretch farther than they used to do, prefloat, and it is all about the time not spent on a delivery truck.

Another major increase in circulation due to floating is that collections are simply better, because patrons themselves play a role in what is offered at any given branch. Mini-trends that might be invisible to librarians' eyes become visible when, for example, all of a sudden books on a particular travel destination, or on urban farming, begin to gather in branches that typically would have held only one or two volumes on the subject. Librarians need to be on their guard. Such shifts do not indicate an imbalance in the collection. Patrons are simply sending a message that this is what they would like more of. A particular part of the city may be all about a new community gardening opportunity. Another may be making blankets for Project Linus. Instead of worrying about having too many books on quilting, librarians need to capitalize on what the invisible patrons are trying to tell them, and they need to alert collection development when they see something like this happening. Knowing about it will allow collection development librarians to determine if this is a long-term, widespread trend, which it often is. These small pools of like materials telegraph much faster what patrons are going to want and need over the coming months than long-term branch profiles ever did, and the nimbleness with which collection development staff can respond can help circulation a great deal.

Floating takes a burden off librarians by constantly refreshing the collection through patron activity. Vendors with products like Collection HQ tout the ability of their systems to make sure shelf-sitters in one branch are swapped out with shelf-sitters in another branch, thus ensuring that libraries get the maximum bang from their collection buck. In a floating collection, this is irrelevant. Patrons themselves provide the churn. Any shelf-sitters that remain get weeded, end of discussion. The items do not sit, there is no need to swap, and that churn, particularly of the higher-circulating items, is also responsible for a long-term circulation increase. The collection is simply fresher and better, and that phenomenon is totally patron driven. Sounds simple, but the effects on the collection are fabulous and long lasting—and fun to watch.

Sometimes staff members are worried about the collection losing its unique identity. What is fascinating about working with a floating collection is that collections clearly become more unique, not less so. And again, that is because of patron activity, not because of anything librarians are doing. If they are smart, librarians are paying attention and asking for more jazz or more canning books from collection development, but they are tailoring the collection to the community by watching the float. And the float is all caused by the patrons themselves. Floating provides a mechanism for the ultimate democratization of the collection. As the patrons bring in what they prefer to read, watch, and listen to (as opposed to what librarians think they should want to read, watch, and listen to) the collections are shaped by the people who are using them. It turns out that when it comes to tweaking the subtle nuances of a subgenre or capturing micro-trends as they break open, patrons are much better at ensuring the most desirable items are available for their fellow branch users than librarians are.

By observing this constant shape-shifting of the collections, librarians are able to capitalize on what the floating collection is telling them, thus optimizing the user experience of that collection, which in turn translates into higher circulation. That kind of immediate responsiveness simply is not available to collection development librarians in a traditionally housed collection. Responsiveness to community need may be, in the end, the most meaningful and long-lasting outcome of floating. Patrons speak loudly and clearly through their use of the collection. Librarians only need to observe and respond in order to capitalize on the intelligence of the float that is presented for their use.

In the initial year or two of floating, keeping up with what types of items are appearing in which branches can be almost a full-time job. This does get easier with time, as profiles and buying patterns are adjusted to meet the patrons' needs, but at the initial go, it can be quite time consuming. As a result, collection development personnel should be aware that if they want to capture the information the float is relaying, they should set aside considerable time for branch visits, communication with branch staff, and adjustments to profiles and orders once they are back in the office. Unlike some issues with floating, such as rebalancing, this honing of the buying process does settle down after a year or so.

PATRON BEHAVIOR, NOT STAFF OPINION

It should not come as a surprise, when a collection begins to float, that what librarians at the local branch level thought their patrons wanted and what the patrons really want are sometimes two very different things. Branch librarians will swear up and down, prefloat, that "romances don't go here" or "I've never been asked for urban fiction/street lit at this branch." What collection development managers know but sometimes struggle to convince their branch colleagues is that certain types of patrons approach staff with questions or for readers' advisory help, and others avoid the librarians like the plague. Therefore, while *staff is absolutely relaying the truth as they experience it,* their experience is limited to those patrons who feel comfortable approaching them and who have the time and the opportunity to do so.

If patrons are calling in dozens of romances under a traditional collection arrangement, those romances are being routed back to the originating branch. The librarians see neither the patron, who goes either straight to the circulation desk or to self-pickup for his or her romances, nor do they see the romances hit the shelves, because the books are returned to the home branch. Therefore, it is easy for branch staff to conclude that the need for romances does not exist. Once floating starts, such invisible patrons become highly visible. All of a sudden, "literary" branches have shelves of romances. Branches whose staffs eschew science fiction and fantasy need a place to shelve significant volumes of it. The same is true for street lit/urban fiction. Staffs need to be prepared for the democratization of their collections. Floating will put on the branch shelves what the community is really reading, not what the librarians think the community is or should be reading; oftentimes there is a significant difference between the two, particularly in regard to genre fiction. As mentioned in earlier chapters, the best indicator of what these invisible patrons are reading, listening to, or viewing is sitting on hold shelves. This is the best predictor of what collection adjustments the branch will have to make once floating starts.

The beauty of a floating collection is that, unlike our staff members, who engage with only a portion of the patrons and can only report on what they see and hear, a floating collection engages with *all* of the patrons, and it reflects back very quickly what patrons want, like, and need. Floating is wonderful for collection development because it makes manifest not only what patrons really want but *where* they want it, and it does so quickly and dramatically. By the same token, weeding is a huge issue in the first year or so after floating, because floating really makes evident what patrons do not want as well as what they do want. After a few months of trying to squeeze items that have floated into a chunk of the collection that is static and unmoving, it becomes evident quickly that even further weeding can be done, to maximize space for the items patrons do want and to minimize the holdings of items that get little or occasional use.

When the evidence of patron behavior begins to aggregate several weeks after floating begins, collection development staff members are able to use that information to reevaluate buying patterns and amounts of items purchased. For some branches, that may mean a greatly enlarged jazz section, the addition of urban lit, or perhaps less of some other topic. Anecdotally, the genre to definitely gain the most shelf space due to floating is romance. Sometimes little respected by librarians, it floats in, time and again, in great waves to those branches where the staff opinion had been firmly held that "our patrons don't read romances." Yes; yes, they do. Lots of them. This is just one illustration of the way in which collection development staff can use what the float shows to increase circulation. So too, in less dramatic fashion, will collection development staff see an increase in other subcategories: the universal popularity of the world wars in history, and/or a call for urban fiction/street lit where they did not know it existed, for instance. But it is romance that usually gains the most. Branches with big romance sections will need bigger ones, and branches with no romance sections will need to find a space for them in a hurry.

For the first time ever, collection development staff has an opportunity to base decision making not on staff opinion but on patron behavior. Staff members report what they know, but the fact of the matter is, they are engaging with only a small percentage of the overall patron base, a fact that historically has skewed the information passed on to collection development librarians. What branch staff members know and observe is helpful, but they do not have the entire picture by any stretch of the imagination. And while collection development librarians may already recognize that fact, it can be quite a jolt after floating begins to discover how large the gap really is between patron behavior and staff opinion in any given branch. Realizing that the prefloat assumptions about what patrons want are just that—assumptions—presents collection development with the daunting but rewarding task of realigning profiles and buying patterns, in order to maximize the materials patrons are seeking and minimize the ones they are not.

CORE COLLECTION AND WEEDING

Besides the daily conversation about rebalancing and helping those branches who are either inundated or are losing too much inventory to the float, there are other long-term issues with which collection development librarians need to concern themselves, such as core collection and weeding. In a traditionally housed collection, branch librarians are aware quickly when their copy of *Little Dorrit* has disappeared for good. In a floating collection, what is not on the shelf or in the collection is much harder to pinpoint.

Cuyahoga County Public Library has developed a core collection marking system that works well to ensure that *Little Dorrit* is always on the shelf. Core collection items are items that have been determined to be essential to collection integrity, or, in some cases, items that are very difficult to obtain, which therefore need to be watched carefully for replacements. Collection development staff identifies "core" items during the ordering or reordering process by typing "CORE" into a field in the vendor interface; this information will be reproduced on the printed purchase order that accompanies the item to cataloging. The cataloging department simply puts "CORE" in the "590" field of the MARC record. When weeding reports are run, they do not include anything where the 590 field equals "CORE." This ensures that core items will not be weeded unless for condition. Additionally, the collection development team runs this list three times a year and checks holdings. Results below a certain predetermined threshold signal more copies to be purchased, which are then marked as "CORE." Other floating libraries rely on staff feedback to know when important titles are missing, but as noted earlier, this can be extremely challenging in a floating environment and often does not occur until patrons have requested a title and come up empty-handed. Creating a core collection marking system that will catch these issues before they happen helps with customer service and circulation.

VETTING OLD EDITIONS IN A FLOATING COLLECTION

When a collection is static, branch librarians can and do keep a weather eye out for condition, age, and edition information. Prefloat, it was rare to find a third edition of a medical book on the shelf if a fourth edition had been issued, for example. Postfloat, such cases are a great deal harder to notice and weed, simply because the collection moves so quickly that it might not be readily apparent that new editions are available and preferable, especially in time-sensitive areas like travel, medicine, and law, to name a few. Floating library systems deal with this "edition issue" in a variety of ways. Some collection development staff call in older editions when a new one is ordered and withdraw them. Other systems do a yearly "age report" for time-sensitive parts of the collection, which lists any editions older than a year or two, depending on the area in question. And of course, branch librarians are invaluable in simply keeping an eye open for these "edition issues," but with more libraries cutting back on staff, the days when people had the time to systematically weed like this are fading fast. It is wise to help the branch librarians by devoting some time and energy to a centralized oversight of some sort at least once year, if possible.

WEEDING A FLOATING COLLECTION

There is one general caveat about weeding a floating collection that is critical. Branch librarians need to resist the urge to weed the collection to fit the space that collection held in a traditionally housed model. When floating begins, librarians often weed popular materials because insufficient shelving has been dedicated in the first place. A common example is cookbooks. In a traditionally housed collection, a shelf range or two may be dedicated to cookbooks. The float begins, and the cookbooks on the hold shelves now come back and live at the branch, greatly impacting that one little range of cookbooks. Many library staff members in the first few months of a float will report that the 641.5 section is "out of control" and weed it vigorously until the cookbooks fit the original shelf range they have always occupied. This can happen with formats like large print or audiobooks as well.

It is sometimes hard for staff to understand that a section is not created by the size of the shelving unit but by the needs and dynamics of that particular collection. Collection development people grasp this immediately because they are used to working with collections in the abstract all the time, constantly shaping a "platonic ideal" of a collection. For branch staffs, the reality is much more concrete, so it is much less likely to occur to them that, rather than weeding the 641.5 section in this example, they should be weeding the underperforming 200 and 300 sections, shifting like crazy and doubling the space for the in-demand cookbooks that have floated in. The patrons are sending the message loud and clear with floating —"more cookbooks!"—and branch staff members just need a word to the wise not to overcorrect when this happens. But not to worry. This will not be a constant shifting nightmare. Once the early changes from floating have been accommodated (more room for cookbooks, large print, whatever), it is a long-term process before patron demand shifts again and the collection must be shifted accordingly. The fact is, the initial changes are correcting for years of incorrect shelving and merchandising allotments, and the float is making that apparent. Once that correction is made in the first few weeks after floating, the collection remains stable for a very long time.

In many ways, weeding a floating collection is different from weeding a traditionally housed collection, but in some very fundamental ways it is exactly the same. Experienced weeders evaluate materials in much the same way they always have. Whether or not to keep the item comes down to the same decision it always has: is it useful in the collection, or not? Librarians who are making these decisions, though, must also now think about the wider context of floating. In many cases, staff members bend way too far backwards trying to preserve materials when floating is new. Surely, they think, someone out there can use this at their branch. That is actually not true. What is true is that if the item were needed elsewhere, it would have already found its way there from patron activity during floating. Floating greatly increases the chances that an item will be called in, shared, or used at a different branch. If it has not been, it is a likely candidate for weeding. But some methods of centralized weeding can help answer such questions and provide that context to make the weeding decisions easier.

If the new work for branch staff members in a floating environment is an aggressive approach to daily weeding, then collection development librarians need to be leading that change. At the same time, repurposing and rebalancing assume a new prominence. Particularly in the early years after a transition to floating, weeding will eliminate a huge percentage of sections that have been overbought in relation to demand over the years. As buying and selection are honed to meet the newly expressed patron preferences evidenced by floating, the underperforming sections need to be weeded harder and harder to make room for in-demand items. A sharp distinction becomes all too apparent between those sections of the collection that are floating so actively (the 641s) and those that are remaining all too stationary (the 800s). Many library systems still devote a disproportionate amount of floor space in the building to nonfiction, despite its relatively poor circulation in comparison with other sections like children's, movies, or fiction. Floating will call the question, make no mistake. Confronted with incontrovertible evidence that their patrons prefer cooking, gardening, and crafts to almost any other nonfiction section, librarians have to make some tough choices about how to position their nonfiction collections, as well as whether or not to give some of that shelving to more popular sections. It makes for an interesting conversation, to say the least.

Centralized Weeding Reports

Many floating systems go to centralized weeding simply because it is harder for branch librarians to know what and what not to weed. If the ILS is capable of generating reports, it is highly desirable that quarterly weeding reports go out to branches. This enables collection development librarians to weed in very creative ways on a system-wide basis, and it saves a lot of time for branch personnel. With floating, an annual or semiannual weed based on low circulation is great. Many systems evaluate for weeding any item that has not circulated at least once in the past calendar year. Some systems increase that to 18 months or 2 years. This approach is very helpful, because the old method of pulling a shelf of books off and evaluating them singly is very difficult to do when the contents of that shelf change every hour of every day due to floating.

Another excellent approach to weeding in a floating collection is to go after specific formats based on age. One of the quarterly weeding reports might cull out any DVD that is over six years old, for example, or any music CD that is over a certain number of years old. What is handy about this is that the buyer for those formats can peruse the reports for anything that should be replaced, so branch personnel can simply withdraw anything on the list.

Pikes Peak "Number System"

Pikes Peak Library District has a great way of helping staff members decide whether to keep copies of materials or to weed them. Sally Houghton, who leads the collection management department, says,

> We have developed a reasonable understanding of the number of copies of a title that are needed in the district collection. When weeding, we check for copies that are in good condition equal to that target figure and get rid of the extras that are on the shelf. This sounds easy and works well for weeding big bestsellers where we have lots of copies in one place at one time and are ready to cut back on the copies that are sitting on the shelf. (Houghton, interview)

Once collection managers have a few months of floating under their belts, this idea works very well and can be communicated easily to branch staff members doing weeding in the branches. Collection development staff certainly buy with those target numbers in mind, so why not also articulate how many to keep? The guideline can be as simple as a list like this:

Bestsellers 0–6 months old—keep all in good condition
Bestsellers 6–12 months old—keep no more than 25
Bestsellers over a year old—keep a dozen

And this could be expanded to other items:

First entry in a mystery series—4 copies
Classic/canon author—4 copies
Perennial school-reading-list author—20 copies

And so on. While it would be impossible to cover every contingency, this technique does give staff good guidelines for a vast majority of the items they encounter while weeding and encourages system-wide weeding. This "sounds easy," as Houghton says, and that's because in a sense, it is not weeding; it is maintaining a minimum number. This method is quick and easy, and staff will clearly understand the guidelines.

The other obvious advantage is that a quick reference guide for multiple copies provides some replacement information, allowing for proactive acquisitions. Houghton comments, "It makes replacement work easier, since we focus on the number of copies in the collection instead of where they are located" (Houghton, interview). So if a branch staffer sees only eight copies of *To Kill a Mockingbird* throughout the system, Houghton and her staff are notified before the student demand hits, and they can ramp up to meet those numbers. The disadvantage of this system is that it is labor intensive on the branch side, in terms of overall workflow. Looking up the total number of copies in the system is time consuming for busy branch staffers and may simply not be practical. But even if some staff in some branches apply this method, it helps provide a measure of "central" oversight, branch by branch.

Weeding Teams

Other library systems with floating collections employ a team approach in their effort to bring centralized oversight to weeding a floating collection. Gwinnett County Public Library is one such library system to use this weeding team approach. Gwinnett's director, Barbara Spruill, spoke in a presentation on floating given at the 2010 Public Library Association (PLA) conference. Spruill explained that because their collection was not weeded vigorously before floating began, it was necessary to form weeding teams to help correct that mistake and catch them up on weeding.

A weeding team is a hand-picked group of experienced weeders who have some sense of the overall collection's needs. They choose a branch and descend as a group, weeding quickly through that branch's collection. The advantage is that local library staffers have fewer weeding decisions to worry about. Just as with completely centralized weeding, the same library staff members are making decisions for the one big collection that floating has created, and so they have a better sense, system-wide, of what should stay and what should be weeded. Since floating creates one collection, having the same small group of people work on weeding throughout the system means that they have a broad current knowledge of both what is being housed in branches and what is needed in branches.

But there are also some disadvantages. The most important one is a lack of accountability for branch staff members. A floating collection means weeding assumes a new importance; it is the new collection work. If a central team assumes that responsibility, branch staffers have less motivation to have their hands in the collection day to day and to know their collection as well.Another disadvantage to team weeding is that the team cannot be everywhere at once. Particularly in the early stages of floating, but ongoing as well, some sections (and some whole branches) will become overcrowded in short order. Waiting for a weeding team to appear sometimes becomes untenable, so staff members weed out of necessity or desperation, and the efficiency of the weeding team concept dissolves in the cold reality of crammed shelves and overflowing backrooms. One possible solution is for branches to continue to weed as best they can and for the weeding teams to focus on only a fraction of the branches, such as those most heavily impacted by the float or those with extremely high circulation but no extra staff or down time in which to accomplish meaningful weeding on an ongoing basis.

Other Best Practices for Weeding a Floating Collection

Here are some good general guidelines.

Weed As the Item Is Checked In

In all but the very busiest of branches, it is worth the time and effort to have circulation and shelving staff attend a refresher workshop about weeding for condition. The reality of a floating collection is that the most-popular, highest-circulating items fly around the system so fast that they are never on the shelf to be evaluated. Therefore, it is critical that circulation staff redouble their efforts to withdraw worn items at the point of return, whether the item has a hold on it or not. Communicate a "weed for condition" mandate to the circulation and shelving staff members. Take 50 items into a workshop setting and have staff vote on what to keep and what to toss, and talk about why. Weeding at the point of check-in is a great defense against the need for heavy weeding in the stacks.

Teach Shelvers to Weed While They Shelve

Shelvers can also engage in a sort of "preweeding" by looking for multiple copies of older bestsellers and by weeding for condition. Shelvers can develop a zero tolerance for multiple copies of bestsellers on the shelves. As they weed, they leave the copy (or two) in best condition on the shelf and pull all the others, placing them on the bottom of their carts for dispensation by the librarians and other qualified staff. Just as it is a simple matter to teach weeding for condition, it is a simple matter to teach shelvers to pull older editions. They approach their shelving with a full cart of returns and are encouraged to return from the stacks with a full or nearly full cart of "preweeded" materials. These materials are then evaluated by qualified staff at service desks between helping patrons, or at other more convenient times. This saves hours of weeding time for busy desk staff, and it helps keep the shelves from being filled with materials that have floated in.

No Single Solution

The first 12 months of the float will see great activity in the collection. A year into floating, the collection will have settled down into very predictable patterns. When that happens, the weeding processes that worked early on may need to be revisited. If there are a great variety of branch sizes and circulation figures, it is highly likely that a combination of several different weeding styles throughout the system will work best. However, as long as weeding is consistently a high priority for branch staff members and collection development librarians, in the end, there is really no wrong way to go about it. If collection development librarians are willing to experiment with selection, allocation, and budget, and if they perceive the value that commitment to in-depth branch visits will gain them, a year or two after floating is initiated, most collection management issues become the new normal.

Reference

Interview

Houghton, Sally. In email interview with the author. August 9, 2010.

EPILOGUE

Floating and the User Experience

Once the transition has been made to a floating collection, it is tempting to declare floating a success and leave it at that, particularly if rebalancing has been anticipated accurately and handled aggressively. Relieved to have the transition to a floating collection behind them and the goals of saving money and labor achieved, many librarians never explore or exploit what can be learned from the patrons' use of the collection—the valuable information that becomes evident once floating is implemented. For collection development librarians, the story is far from over. And for staff members concerned with readers' advisory, displays and merchandising, or user design and experience, much thoughtful work lies ahead in the months and years after floating has been launched. It is important to realize that floating continues to reveal information about patron behavior perpetually, not just in the year or two after floating begins. A floating collection, observed carefully, can help librarians understand patron activity across three levels of library work:

- Collection work—selection, core collection and/or replacement work, budgeting, distribution, weeding, and repurposing of excess materials

- Facility planning and design—repurposing of traditional "academic" shelving arrangements to more relevant shelving that allows for flexibility and expansion in areas of changing patron interests, as well as more meaningful and useful public space overall

- Readers' advisory, merchandising and displays, and programming

If librarians throughout the system look closely at what materials float (and what materials do not) as floating matures, they can improve the patrons' experience in all of these areas.

FLOATING AND THE USER EXPERIENCE

"User experience" is a phrase that originated with web designers to refer to the overall engagement a patron or participant had—or failed to have—with a website. It is a concept related to strong and intentional customer service, but it goes a step further. From the approach/discovery phase to the conclusion of a visit to a website, user experience designers carefully note where patrons click and what aspects of the site they avoid. If the designers have done a good job, users will be back for a return visit to that site. If they have not, users will be off to search for an easier way to accomplish what they needed to do. At its most basic, user experience theory forces designers to think the way a user thinks, and every decision is based on the actual users' behavior. Aaron Schmidt, writing about user experience for *Library Journal* defined it as "arranging the elements of a product or service to optimize how people will interact with it." Schmidt goes on to say,

> The secret here is not to think of library patrons, users, or customers; we need to think of people. We need to consider their lives and what they are trying to accomplish. This act, which can only be done by cultivating the skill of empathy, is the most important—and perhaps the most difficult—part of user experience design. (Schmidt, article)

How is user experience relevant to floating collections? Once items are moved to collections in particular branches, patron activity fine-tunes the placement of those materials. By placing holds and returning items to a local branch, patrons are taking user experience—and design—of the collection into their own hands. A floating collection has an intelligence and an energy that originate from the patrons' activity. Functioning like the best artificial intelligence in website design, the floating collection constantly reshapes itself to be better, timelier, and more desirable with each hold that is placed. By observing changes in what patrons have called in and moved about, librarians can extrapolate information and make very educated guesses about what their patron base is looking for at any given time.

COLLECTION WORK AND THE USER EXPERIENCE

Patrons interested in a piece of folk music they heard at a neighborhood festival can place a hold, pick up the item, and return it. Now that very specific piece of music is in the right place at the right time for the next patron, who just happened to hear the same band perform. If every library employee involved in branch work or collection development could attend every church book discussion, every festival, wedding, school play; read every blog; see every film; and watch every TV show, they still could not rival the ability of the patrons to manipulate the collection in such a way as to instantaneously reflect current interests and tastes. "Fine-tuning" does not begin to describe the optimal level of patron service a floating collection can deliver. Floating collections can take the guesswork out of collection development, but only if collection development staff members are primed and ready to absorb and capitalize on the information. In some ways, the intelligence waiting to be gathered through a floating collection makes the job easier, but it also requires a lot more vigilance to follow trends and patterns as they emerge and to respond quickly and effectively to what the patrons are trying to say through their use of the collection. First and most obviously, the patron activity in a floating collection, as noted earlier, can point out what patrons want and what they do not. No matter how well weeded a collection is, a year or so after floating, many libraries take on a second major weed, this time because the portion of the collection that has not floated, but has remained stolidly on the shelves, needs to be cleared away to make room for more of what the patrons are taking out. A great deal of this second wave of weeding is to get rid of items many librarians considered a "must-have"—not necessarily core collection, but things that patrons might ask for. As has been talked about at some length in the library literature over the past few years, "might ask for" is a luxury almost no library can afford. If the patrons have not used an item or a part of the collection for a year or so, it really must go, and it becomes obvious where those dusty corners are. Similarly, hot items like cookbooks and romances are in great demand and are the logical place for more collection dollars. Simply put, if a part of the collection moves swiftly and is in near-constant demand, chances are that the library system is missing the boat and not adequately fulfilling that demand.

FACILITY PLANNING AND DESIGN AND THE USER EXPERIENCE

Although the effect of floating on library buildings has been little talked about, this is an area of enormous opportunity for library planners who are willing and financially able to take advantage of it. One of the biggest mistakes libraries make is to not inform those responsible for buildings and layouts of shelving ranges that floating will change the form and shape of the actual collection. This is usually a sin of omission, as many implementers of floating do not realize for themselves the dramatic changes that can take place in branches. For most branches, the changes will be similar: large prints and books on CD need more space, as do romances and cookbooks. But particularly for the large have-not branches, oftentimes the main library, facility planners need to be poised to make immediate changes—as soon as 60 to 90 days after floating begins. Sometimes librarians at the main library and other large have-not branches think the books and other items will come back, and they hesitate to take action. Those items will not come back. The float never lies in this regard—once a "have-not," always a have-not. Instead, facility planners should be condensing collections and pulling down shelving ranges, opening up space for laptop users or soft seating for readers. Facility designers should try designing a new user experience to be put into place after floating starts, so that rather than disappointed patrons facing empty stacks, the library system has delighted patrons using the new computers or enjoying studying as a group. A time when the collection is literally redesigning itself is a fabulous opportunity to redesign the user experience of the building. For most libraries, this large redesign for the "have-nots" is a one-time occurrence, but flexible shelving takes on a new importance for the more minor, ongoing changes that develop. At least once a year, branch managers, collection development personnel, and facility planners should look at ways in which the user experience of the library can be enhanced by changing the layout, discontinuing some formats, and expanding others. The reward is ever-increasing circulation; users respond when their message is received and acted upon.

READERS' ADVISORY, MERCHANDISING/ DISPLAYS, PROGRAMMING AND THE USER EXPERIENCE

It is not uncommon for librarians to read what they enjoy reading and then pass those books along to their patrons. In a floating collection, librarians have a unique opportunity to turn this part of the user experience on its head, making "readers' advisory" precisely that. Rather than reading the books that are getting starred reviews and then pressing them onto their readers, readers' advisory librarians can "read the float" and design a user experience that gives the readers more of what they want, not more of what librarians think they should want. Librarians who are willing to think about what their users are reading right now will see those items wash in with the float, and if they are smart, they will start reading right along with their patrons. Doing so shows a respect and an awareness that is difficult to manifest in a traditionally housed collection. If those items can form the themes of displays and the basis of programming, librarians can continue to heighten the user experience on those levels as well. What kinds of books are in the branches that were not there a few weeks ago? What subjects? What authors? It helps to make displays and merchandising more relevant and programming more surefire; all librarians have to do is walk their shelves and pay attention. It is as simple as that.

CONCLUSION

Floating collections can help librarians to understand more clearly what patrons want. This is on top of the other advantages of floating, such as saving money, saving wear and tear on materials and people, increasing circulation, and forcing librarians to practice better and more vigilant collection practices. And although floating causes rebalancing to become the new normal, with strong communication, a willingness to be flexible and try new approaches, and frequent branch visits, this cost of doing business pales in comparison to the benefits that a floating collection can provide. For the library systems that have stepped forward with floating, the benefits outweigh any challenges, and for library systems considering floating, there are a myriad of ways in which floating can be adapted to make the most of any library system's resources.

Reference

Article

Schmidt, Aaron. "The User Experience." *Library Journal* 135, no. 1 (2010): 28–9.

10 Great Reasons to Float

THE ADVANTAGES AND DISADVANTAGES OF A FLOATING COLLECTION

It is often assumed that the only reason for floating a library collection is to save money. While floating definitely saves money, there are other excellent reasons to float. Here are 10 great reasons that dozens of public libraries have embraced floating and never looked back.

1. *Floating saves a lot of money.* Floating saves money on delivery costs, usually in direct relation to the geographic size of the systems. In a city-wide or county-wide system that covers a sprawling geographic area, floating can save a lot of money, but even for systems without big geographic challenges, floating still reduces delivery and material handling costs. Fewer trucks mean less fuel, mileage, and vehicle maintenance. If delivery is contracted out it saves on contract costs for that service.

2. *Floating pleases patrons and increases circulation,* for these reasons:

   a. Constantly refreshed collections mean better browsing, more opportunities for readers' advisory and merchandising, and increased circulation.

   b. Patrons will swear that more items are being purchased when in fact the opposite is true. Fewer copies need to be purchased because materials spend more time out of delivery trucks and more time on shelves, and because copies can land where they are most needed, making items readily available for circulation.

c. Patrons who forget to pick up their held items in a timely fashion are *delighted* to find that the item has not shipped back to an owning branch but is instead awaiting them in their home branch collection. This reduces patron frustration as well as staff time that would have been needed to reorder the item and send it a second time.

3. *Floating saves a lot of time.* Circulation staff members love floating collections, because hours spent routing items back to their owning locations are eliminated, freeing up staff time for more important, less repetitive tasks.

4. *Floating forces improved collection management:* selection, weeding, and responsiveness to patrons' preferences and needs come to the fore when working with a floating collection. Beginning and maintaining a floating collection has many positive side effects on collection work itself.

5. *Floating saves wear and tear on staff and on items.* Fewer delivery bins to toss onto trucks equal less wear and tear ergonomically on staff members, less unnecessary handling of items, less wear and tear on the materials themselves.

6. *Floating saves paging/shelving time, providing faster customer service.* In a better-weeded, better-maintained, and more active collection, less time is spent hunting items to be sent to a patron at another branch.

7. *Floating saves a lot of money in collection budgets.* No longer does every small branch or every heavily hit branch require a copy of every title. Instead, a smaller number of items can serve to enrich many branch collections as they travel throughout the system.

8. *Floating saves time in processing materials.* Because labels are centralized and items do not have to be marked with owning location labels, processing time and costs are reduced whether done in-house or through a vendor.

9. *Buying is based on patron behavior, not staff opinion.* Floating helps to perfect collection development because patrons are participating in the process. Private industry spends millions of dollars for marketing information about customer tastes. With a floating collection, patrons make their selections as they check out materials and then *return* the choices they have made, thus giving their librarians precious information about their "buying" habits, needs, and preferences. All the staff has to do is look.

10. *Floating enriches the entire collection and helps the invisible customer become visible.* Big branches have to "share the wealth" and let their premium resources reside in the less-rarified world of busy

smaller branches. Whether selection is centralized or not, floating helps librarians to recognize groups, minorities, and cultures who are using the library. These customers may have been previously ignored, consciously or not, by librarians who tend to see patrons with similar values and the cultural norms more closely aligned with their own. By pooling their selections in branches that may not have previously recognized the extent of the demand, romance readers, gay/lesbian readers, street lit readers, and others can make their voices heard, simply by making their choices visible. Floating collections are a vote for democracy in a selection system long dominated by white middle class women of a certain age, as less-mainstream collections gather in numbers too great to ignore.

Partial List of Floating Libraries

Arizona
   Pima County Public Library
California
   San Jose Public Library
   San Mateo County Library
Colorado
   Arapahoe Library District
   Denver Public Library
   Pikes Peak Library District
Florida
   Collier County Public Library
   Orange County Library District
   Sarasota County Library System
Indiana
   Indianapolis-Marion County Public Library
Maryland
   Baltimore County Public Library
Michigan
   Kent District Library
   Monroe County Library System
Minnesota
   Hennepin County Library
Missouri
   Springfield-Greene County Library District
Nebraska
   Omaha Public Library

Nevada

Henderson District Public Libraries

Las Vegas-Clark County Library District

Washoe County Library System

New Mexico

Albuquerque-Bernalillo County Library System

North Carolina

Charlotte Mecklenburg Library

Ohio

Akron-Summit County Public Library

Columbus Metropolitan Library

Cuyahoga County Public Library

Dayton Metro Library

Medina County District Library

Public Library of Cincinnati and Hamilton County

Stark County District Library

Toledo-Lucas County Public Library

Oregon

Multnomah County Library

Virginia

Henrico County Public Library

Prince William Public Library System

Washington

Timberland Regional Library

APPENDIX C

Floating Risk Evaluation

Rate the library's situation by assigning the following numbers to the four statements below.

1 = Not at all

2 = Somewhat

3 = Definitely

4 = Very much

____ The library needs to save money.

____ The library needs to improve circulation.

____ An imbalanced collection in a minority of the branches and the staff dissatisfaction connected with it would be the type of disruption the library would be prepared to handle.

____ If related questions arise about how the library handles the collection, the library would be able to tolerate discussion of its internal logistics and to consider options.

Total score _____

Scoring:
A score of 4–8 indicates either that the need for a floating collection is great, but the risks associated with it may not be worth it, or that the need is moderate, as is the risk tolerance.

A score of 9–16 indicates that the need for a floating collection is moderate to great, and the risk tolerance of the library allows for serious consideration of a change to a floating collection.

APPENDIX D

Deciding to Float: Discussion Questions

The following questions are an excellent starting point for decision makers trying to evaluate whether or not floating is right for their library system. Also, these questions can easily be converted to ask a currently floating "like library" to convey their experience—for example, "How did floating affect your staff?" and so on.

1. Does the library need to save money?
2. Does the library need to improve circulation?
3. Floating will create an imbalanced collection in a minority of the branches and create staff dissatisfaction connected with it. Is this something the library would be prepared to handle?
4. Floating creates related questions about how the library handles the collection. When those questions arise, would the library be able to tolerate discussion of its internal logistics and consider options?
5. Can the library steer a middle course and float only part of the collection? Would it be worth it?
6. How will floating affect the patrons?
7. How will floating affect circulation?
8. How will floating affect the staff?
9. How will floating affect the collection?
10. How will floating affect fellow consortia libraries?

11. Are there other mind-bending, paradigm-shifting, major upheavals taking place?

12. Have like libraries converted successfully to floating?

13. What are the hidden costs or risks?

14. Is now the right time to centralize?

15. What is the worst-case scenario?

16. Who should be involved if the decision is made to move forward?

17. Will the entire collection float? If not, what parts should not?

APPENDIX E

Chart for Prefloat Branch Visits

Branch Name	Prefloat Percentage	Hold Shelf #	Location Info	Weeding Status
Clarkson				
Main Library				
Fuller				
Exton				
Ridge Park				
Greensburg				
Dover				
Carnegie				

APPENDIX F

Staff Communication

FREQUENTLY ASKED QUESTIONS

1. How will I know what is in my collection day to day if it changes all the time?

   One of the biggest losses for staff members is the comfort of knowing precisely what is in their collection day to day. Staff members will often say, "But I have my collection memorized!" And while that certainly makes their job easier, the downside is that the patrons likely have it memorized as well, making for a very dull browsing experience. However, this loss is very real to staff members, many of whom, in the days before central selection, spent years of their careers helping to shape their branch collection. In some systems, they may still be selecting in the branch. Although this fear is probably the most deeply held, the good news is that it is also the most easily dissipated. Once floating has begun, staff members see for themselves that their entire collection does not change overnight. Because floating activity correlates directly with circulation activity, the collections for movies and pop music do indeed change overnight, and popular new books come and go at the blink of an eye. And staff members are correct. It takes hard work and dedication to keep up with those constantly refreshed collections. But adult fiction, nonfiction, and children's collections are much lower circulating, and therefore, they are more stable. For most branches, it takes months and months for a majority of those materials to float in and out. (This is an excellent example of a concern that can be quickly put to rest by inviting librarians and other staff members from a nearby floating system to answer questions—more on that below.)

2. What if my very important local history book floats away and someone weeds it in error?

   Many staff members' concerns focus around the perceived incompetence of their colleagues. This is most often an attitude displayed by main branch personnel toward their colleagues in the branches. Staff members at the main library will be delighted to discover once floating begins that branch personnel are as adept at identifying important, one-of-a-kind sources as they themselves are. (The float team, per the discussion below, can also choose to make some holdings not float, assuming there is a legitimate concern.) Staff members should be encouraged to bring examples of such materials to staff meetings on floating for discussion.

3. What if patrons at my branch have cards that are too compromised to place holds? We will not get any books!

   This is a serious concern, not just for staff members but for the float team and decision makers. After all, movement in a floating collection relies on patron activity—checkouts, drop-offs, holds, and so on. The concern is that in branches where patrons cannot or choose not to place holds, a disproportionately low amount of floating will occur. Surprisingly, this actually does not come to pass. While branches with tech-savvy patrons who place holds certainly have a higher float percentage, card-challenged branches experience the same float percentage one would expect for a non-tech-savvy branch of any kind. For all the concerns about this issue, it simply has not happened to any major degree. One explanation may be that because the staff members have a higher rate of contact with the card-challenged patrons, those patrons who do check out and return a high volume of materials are less visible to staff members, so it feels as though "all" patrons have cards with issues and avoid placing holds, while in fact, this simply is not true.

4. I am afraid my branch collection will not be unique anymore.

   Actually, nothing could be farther from the truth, although this is hard for staff members to understand until they actually see it take place. Because floating allows patrons to participate in collection development, customer activity brings in scores of wonderful materials that change and focus the collection more every day. Floating actually makes collections *more* unique to the needs of their particular patrons and neighborhoods, in ways the most talented collection development people in the world could not hope to duplicate. Floating makes collections more unique, not less.

5. Lots of people drop stuff off here. We are going to be buried in materials!

Ah, the Myth of the Drop-Off Branch. It is interesting how passionately staff members and branch managers believe this, even when it runs completely counter to common sense. Branch managers in hard-to-reach bedroom communities with no commuter traffic will swear up and down that they are a drop-off for neighboring larger, busy branches and predict doom and gloom for floating's effect on their branch. Just as interestingly, branch managers in branches that are serious drop-off branches seem blithely unconcerned. (The right people never believe the Drop-Off Myths!) As previously discussed, there are simple and reliable methods to predict how, when, and where the float will hit, based on existing patron behavior, not staff opinion. Once confronted with these facts and educated about where their metrics fall within the larger picture of the other branches, branch managers and staff members may be skeptical, but at least they will know that the float team has things well in hand. Just as importantly, if there are branch managers and staff members at potentially heavily hit branches who are rather blasé about their impending status, seeing how high they are on these measures can help them to realize that they'd better be prepared for some serious work flow changes.

6. What if there is a school assignment on giraffes and all "my" giraffe books have floated away?

This is a common (and very deep) concern for children's librarians. As previously noted, children's nonfiction, which is of course assignment related (and therefore the cause for the concern), floats the least because it almost always circulates the least. Children's librarians are extremely anxious about this type of issue, because of course their patrons are counting on those materials being there. It helps to remind them that in most systems, the collection with the least amount of float is children's nonfiction. Once again, this fear dissipates almost immediately when floating begins, and disaster fails to strike as collections remain stable. Also, children's librarians should be encouraged to create their own "customer activity." If they know an assignment on butterflies is approaching, they can use a staff card to call in the needed books and other materials. Creating a little "man-made" float is a perfectly legitimate thing to do and is an aid to customer service. Otherwise, butterfly books can be called in for patrons individually, and the float will reverse itself, but most librarians like being ahead of the assignment curve.

7. What if I call in books for a book discussion group and they all end up on our shelves?

Again, it is amazing how common this question was across systems that floated. The correct answer is, "Don't worry about it." Given time, floating will correct this minor overage in the system as other patrons place holds on those volumes and float them out. It does not matter if every single copy of *Water for Elephants* ends up at one branch. But for whatever reason, this little side note to floating causes incredible anxiety for some staff members. Therefore, most systems encourage staff members to simply redistribute those books to other branches, not because it will harm the collection in any way if they stay, but to assuage the upset surrounding this issue.

Communication Timeline

60–90 days before floating begins	**Workshop—half day for all staff to introduce floating**	Floating explained; guests from floating systems introduced for Q and A; questions and concerns answered; timeline for preparation and implementation for floating distributed.
Immediately following staff workshop	**Wiki, blog, or Q and A spot on staff intranet.**	Accessible to all staff members; manned by float team; for staff Q and A and general information posting.
45–60 days before floating begins	**Branch visits**	Obtain metrics to predict floating's effect on each branch; meet with branch managers, head librarians in adult and children's areas, circulation supervisors, and the supervisor of the shelvers/pages.
45 days before floating begins	**Targeted meetings for weeding or shelving catch-up**	Department heads, branch managers, any other leadership involved in getting the branches weeded or caught up on shelving.
Floating begins!!	**Wiki, blog, Q and A spot**	Float team should be posting common concerns, questions, as well as successes reported on branch visits.
3–6 weeks after floating begins	**Postfloat branch visits**	Obtain the postfloat percentage; meet with branch managers and other key personnel to answer questions and help to problem-solve. Identify branches to be included in rebalancing work group.
6 weeks after floating begins	**Rebalancing work group**	Float team and representatives from the heavily hit and "have-not" branches.

APPENDIX H

Sample 24-Door-to-Floor Cart Tag

24-Door-to-Floor Cart Tag

Date _____
  (noted by circulation clerk)

Cart shelved by _____
  (shelver's name or initials)

Type of Cart _____
  (DVD, kids' nonfiction, new books, music CD, etc.)

Cart begun: Day _____ Time _____

Cart completed: Day _____ Time _____

Shelver's Notes:
Interruptions—meeting room set up, snow shoveling, break time, etc.

Problems encountered—800s need shelf read, out of room in audiobooks, etc.

Bibliography

ARTICLES

Cress, Ann. "The Latest Wave." *Library Journal* 129, no. 16 (2004): 48–50.

Hilyard, N. B., ed. "Take the Plunge! Implementing Floating Collections in Your Library System." *Public Libraries, Perspectives*, May/June 2012, 13–20.

Schmidt, Aaron. "The User Experience." *Library Journal* 135, no. 1 (2010): 28–9.

BOOKS

Alabaster, Carol. *Developing an Outstanding Core Collection: A Guide for Libraries*. Chicago: American Library Association. 2002.

American Library Directory 2013–2014. 66th ed. 2 vols. Medford, NJ: Information Today, Inc., 2013.

Bridges, William. *Managing Transitions: Making the Most of Change*. 3rd ed. Philadelphia: Da Capo Lifelong Books, 2009.

Index

72; communication, 71–72, 75; percentage, 34, 55, 72–73

Prefloat percentage, 33–35, 37–38, 115

Preparation, for float, 59–70; branch location and, 38–40; branch size and circulation rank, 29–30; hold shelves, 35–38; prediction and, 29–45; prefloat percentage, 33–35, 37–38; reports and statistics in, 32–33; shelving practices and, 59–60, 61–70; shifting and "two fists" rule, 69–70; success in, 32–33; weeding in, 40–45, 60, 68–70

Processing, centralized, 26

Public floating libraries, list of, 7–9, 110–11

Readers' advisory, 104

Rebalancing, 9, 16, 24, 95; automated or vendor solutions to, 78; by-the-bin method, 78–79; central posting board or wiki, 79–80; email communication for, 76–77, 80; "have-not" branches and, 7, 78, 80; main library and, 4, 7, 55, 74; postfloat plans for, 74, 75–80; send lists for, 80; staff morale and, 48; weeding and, 26, 44; work group for, 55–56

Risk evaluation, 16, 17, 27–28

Romance fiction, 91, 92

Schmidt, Aaron, 102

School libraries, 10

Selection, 87–88, 95 (see also Collection development staff); budget and, 81–85; centralizing, 24–25, 48, 81; circulation and, 83; errors in, 23

Shelving practices, 59–60, 61–70, 94, 104; cart tags, 64, 67, 121; circulation and, 61, 63–64, 67; popular (hot) items and, 60, 61, 62, 63–64, 68; rebalancing and, 78; shifting and "two fists" rule, 69–70;

24-door-to-floor method, 63–68; weeding and, 60, 68–70, 98

Special collections, 3, 27, 41, 54, 59, 60

Spruill, Barbara, 97

Staff communication. See Communication, with staff

Staff members. See Branch staff; Collection development staff; Library staff

Timeline, 12, 42; for staff communication, 52–53, 120

Time saving, 5, 48; in processing materials, 6, 108

"Too Much, Not Enough" board, 79–80

Triple I. See Innovative Interfaces, Inc.

24-Door-to-Floor shelving method, 63–68; cart tags, 64, 65, 67, 121

Upfold, Michael, 9

User experience, 11, 101–5. See also Patrons, floating and

Visibility, of patrons, 6, 31, 35–38, 89, 91, 108

Weeding, 56, 82, 91, 93–99; best practices for, 95–99; branch staff and, 22, 93, 94; centralization of, 25–26, 42, 81, 95–96, 97; circulation activity and, 20–21; core collection and, 92–93; "ghost" items, 42, 69; increased circulation and, 36; "ninja" weeding, 66; Pikes Peak "Number System," 96–97; prior to floating, 23, 55, 68–70; second wave of, 103; of shelf-sitters, 89; shelving practices and, 60, 68–70, 98; teams for, 97–98

Weeding reports, 40–45, 69, 93, 95–96

Wiki, 79–80

Workflow, of library staff, 13, 47, 48, 72, 81 (see also Rebalancing; Weeding); drop-off branch myth and, 51; weeding and, 22, 97

About the Author

Photo by David Bullock.

WENDY K. BARTLETT is the collection development manager for the Cuyahoga County Public Library system outside of Cleveland, Ohio. Opinions expressed in this book belong to the author and do not necessarily represent the opinions of the Cuyahoga County Public Library. Before joining the collection development department, she was the branch manager for the Beachwood branch of the Cuyahoga County Public Library, and previous to that she was the assistant director of the Kent Free Library in Kent, Ohio. She is the author of "Floating Collections: Perspectives from a Public Librarian," in *Rethinking Collection Development and Management*, edited by Becky Albitz, Christine Avery, and Diane Zabel.

PROFESSIONAL COLLECTION

R 025.21 BARTLETT
Bartlett, Wendy K.
Floating collections :
R2003327133 CENTRAL

CPSIA information
Printed in the USA
BVOW04s135111

355919BV

Atlanta-Fulton Public Library

1598 847437